PENGUIN BOOKS

K
Y
L
I
E

Dino Scatena is the music editor of Sydney's *Daily Telegraph* newspaper. A journalism graduate from the Royal Melbourne Institute of Technology, he has been a high-profile commentator on pop culture in Australia for close to a decade and was formerly music editor of the Australian edition of *Rolling Stone*. The second child of Italian immigrants, Dino was born in the same city and year (Melbourne, 1968) as Kylie Minogue.

AN
UNAUTHORISED
BIOGRAPHY

KYLIE

DINO
SCATENA

PENGUIN BOOKS

Penguin Books Australia Ltd
487 Maroondah Highway, PO Box 257
Ringwood, Victoria 3134, Australia
Penguin Books Ltd
Harmondsworth, Middlesex, England
Penguin Putnam Inc.
375 Hudson Street, New York, New York 10014, USA
Penguin Books Canada Limited
10 Alcorn Avenue, Toronto, Ontario, Canada M4V 3B2
Penguin Books (NZ) Ltd
Cnr Rosedale and Airborne Roads, Albany, Auckland, New Zealand
Penguin Books (South Africa) (Pty) Ltd
24 Sturdee Avenue, Rosebank, Johannesburg 2196, South Africa
Penguin Books India (P) Ltd
11, Community Centre, Panchsheel Park, New Delhi 110 017, India

First published by Penguin Books Australia 1997

10 9 8 7 6 5 4 3 2

Designed by Glenn Thomas, Penguin Design Studio
Typeset in 10/15pt Rotis by Midland Typesetters, Maryborough, Victoria
Printed and bound in Australia by McPherson's Printing Group, Maryborough,
Victoria

National Library of Australia
Cataloguing-in-Publication data:

Scatena, Dino, 1968– .
  Kylie: an unauthorised biography.

  Bibliography.
  Includes index.
  ISBN 0 14 025328 9.

  1. Minogue, Kylie, 1968– . 2. Television actors and actresses – Australia –
Biography. 3. Siingers – Australia – Biography. I. Title.

791.45092

www.penguin.com.au

contents

KYLIE IS A SUPERSTAR. TO SOME FOLK AROUND THE PLANET, SHE IS AN IDOL, AN ICON.

PREFACE

in the image of kylie

This story is about the making of Kylie. It's the breakdown of a modern pop phenomenon, traced from the drawing board of a TV network's promotions office all the way to the top of the world's record charts. It's a behind-the-scenes view of a massive marketing campaign driven by lies, half-truths and make-believe. It exposes Kylie's creators and the intricate link of agents who have played a part in the forging of modern pop history.

But this book is also about a fairytale starring the real-life adventures of a shy, blonde-and-blue-eyed girl who once lived in a happy home at the bottom of the world.

This, boys and girls, is the extraordinary tale of Kylie Ann Minogue.

Since 1992, Kylie has released only one studio album, 1994's *Kylie Minogue*. At last report, Kylie was leisurely working on new songs with the producers, Brothers in Rhythm, for an album called *The Impossible Princess*, which will be released in late 1997. As an actress during this same period, Kylie has only had two minor, supporting roles in a couple of forgettable B-grade Hollywood flicks – 1994's *Street Fighter* and 1995's *Bio Dome*.

Aside from some limited promotional work for these projects, Kylie has basically left herself a lot of spare time to do nothing in particular – hang out in her apartment in the London suburb of

Chelsea, visit the family in Australia, drop over to Paris for dinner, whatever. The fact is, Kylie doesn't care much for work anymore. It's hardly surprising, considering there was a time not that long ago when Kylie did nothing but work.

Back in the late eighties – when she was literally the biggest pop star in the UK, Australia, Europe and Asia – Kylie's intense promotional schedules rarely allowed for a single day off. It was a relentless publicity campaign of media interviews and international engagements, photo shoots and staged public appearances. That went on for over three years.

It's what made Kylie a superstar, helping the former TV soap actress sell an estimated thirteen million albums and over twenty million singles. But it also deprived Kylie of a big chunk of her youth, and on occasions pushed her to the brink of a nervous breakdown.

Kylie has spent the last few years making up for lost time. She may not sell anywhere near the number of records she used to in the old days, but that doesn't bother her in the slightest. Kylie is an 'artist' now – it's her prerogative to indulge in the freedoms the world grants its superstar artists.

The Kylie of today is far removed from the pre-adolescent incarnation that day-dreamed about being a famous singer. That little buck-toothed kid knew nothing about real fame: her only wish was to be like Olivia Newton-John, up there on the screen, dancing with John Travolta in *Grease*. Today's Kylie, on the other hand, knows everything about fame, has personally experienced every high and low it has to offer.

This book is a record of the private and public moments that changed Kylie Ann Minogue from the schoolgirl to the superstar. Much of the action takes place before Kylie's big chill-out in 1992. If you already know anything about Kylie, some of the stories will be familiar – a few have left an indelible mark on popular culture.

This book is a celebration of all things Kylie, a salute to a bizarre and wonderful career. It's also an attempt to gain a better understanding of Kylie herself, a more honest representation. It is an effort to imagine what the artist's metamorphosis must have looked like from her side of the screen.

Terry Blamey, Kylie's personal manager since 1987, wanted nothing to do with this book. Blamey was happy to discuss the idea of a completely authorised Kylie biography – one in which he'd choose which details to omit – but there was no way his prized client wanted anything to do with an independent biography. 'I don't trust it,' Blamey slung at your narrator, branding this book 'not a reputable work' and a 'slander campaign' even before the first word had been written. This was to be expected – it's the standard rhetoric that's been flung at anyone who's ever been caught snooping around the corridors of Kylie the Superstar Inc.

Blamey has long trumpeted the claim that over 70 per cent of everything ever reported about his girl has been invented, a fabrication of Kylie's eternal arch-enemy, the media.

Indeed, Kylie's relationship with the international media has bordered on the surreal at times, and, yes, there's been a lot of misinformation bandied about (the overall fiction factor is probably closer to 35–40 per cent). But the fact is, Blamey and others in the Kylie camp – including the woman herself – have always been a main source of the reality morphs. Certainly, Kylie and her people have never been shy about lying to the media when it's suited them.

The deception started even before Blamey came on the scene. It dates back to early 1986, when Kylie, a seventeen-year-old novice actor just out of high school, took on the role of the emotionally intense girl-next-door mechanic, Charlene Mitchell, in the Australian television soap, *Neighbours*. Something strange and inexplicable followed – an illustration of the bizarre nature of television.

In a little over a year after Kylie joined the cast, *Neighbours* – a mundane, low-budget, five-night-a-week drama replicating life in suburbia – was drawing millions of viewers across Australia, and later in the UK. The simple reason for *Neighbours'* success was Kylie. Or, more precisely, Kylie and Jason Donovan.

Jason, who played the character of schoolboy Scott Robinson in *Neighbours*, became the Mickey to Kylie's Minnie. On-screen, *Neighbours* rooted itself in the highs and lows provided by Charlene and Scott's chaste teenage romance. Off-screen, the young actors had become lovers from virtually the moment they met.

But nobody was to know that. Literally. The producers of *Neighbours* bullied the two kids into keeping their puppy-love completely under wraps. As the show's ratings began to sky-rocket, Kylie and Jason were constantly reminded that if their relationship became public knowledge, *Neighbours* would be ruined. That meant Charlene and Scott would be killed, and Kylie and Jason's careers buried along with the bodies.

The producers' threat turned out to be a stroke of marketing genius. When Kylie and Jason eventually left *Neighbours* to become instant pop stars, the pair's music producers insisted they persist with the same campaign. For the duration of their four-year relationship, Kylie and Jason may have been sharing the same bed most nights, but in daylight hours they obligingly played out the image of two sweet, clean-cut kids devoid of genitalia.

Mainstream media usually discards such frivolous concerns about young stars as fodder for the teen mags. But Kylie and Jason's immense popularity, coupled with the intrigue stirred by their refusal to confirm any real-life romance, quickly snowballed into an absurd media frenzy, one which would rival the Di-and-Chuck fling for column inches in the Australian and British press for much of the late eighties.

The whole thing was gloriously banal – all this focus on two very average, mildly talented kids from suburbia who had nothing more to say about life other than the same old lie: 'We're just good friends.'

But it was a line that would help make *Neighbours* a hit, and would play a factor in selling lots of records. And it taught everyone involved with Kylie and Jason a valuable skill: media manipulation. In the hectic years to follow, those driving the Kylie phenomenon would refine that skill into a modern art form.

'It wouldn't matter if they took a photo of me naked in a glass box in the middle of the city, they can't get inside the real me,' said the nineteen-year-old Kylie in 1988 soon after photos of her topless on a beach with 'good friend' Jason Donovan were splashed across newspapers in Australia and the UK.

It must have been a strange view for Kylie, inside that box looking out.

Asked recently what she'd meant by those words, Kylie just shrugged and said she didn't remember ever saying them. 'It was probably just made up.'

Perhaps it was that topless photo incident that set off the cloud of misinformation that would hide the real Kylie for so long.

Now, nearly ten years down the track, not even the cruellest words are likely to scar Kylie. She's heard it all before. So has everybody else. But the people around her insist on remaining paranoid. And fair enough, too. Both Kylie and Terry Blamey have been through the press wringer countless times.

Since those insane days of the late eighties, Blamey has learned how to control and manipulate the media so that it works in his client's favour. For a long time now, everything you've known about Kylie is only what Kylie and Blamey decided you should know. And usually that information is sold to the highest bidder. Photos cost extra.

It's no surprise that Blamey wanted nothing to do with this book. What could possibly be gained when so much work has been put in by so many people over so many years to make the image of Kylie perfect? As producer Peter Waterman said in reference to Kylie's unchanging pop formula in those early days, 'If it ain't broke, don't fix it.'

Kylie wasn't made available to offer any direct comment on this version of her life. Blamey made it clear that he believed Kylie's story couldn't be written without his assistance. Well, Blamey was wrong, but the absence of Ms Minogue's personal blessing for the project certainly didn't help matters.

Kylie's done a lot of talking on the record over the years – talking about yourself is one of the main requirements of the pop-star gig – and there are dust specks of truth scattered throughout her huge international file of press clippings and television interviews. Even Kylie the 'utter-professional' couldn't keep her guard up all the time.

Without the nod from Kylie, however, several people who were closest to her at different points of her life also refused to contribute anything to this version of events. Notable absentees include Jason Donovan and Michael Hutchence. Fortunately, like Kylie, they've also said a lot through the course of hundreds of interviews.

Nearly everyone who's ever got close to Kylie has, at some point, been offered huge sums of money to spill a few scandalous beans. Some chose to take that blood money years ago and told all of what little they knew.

Others, in unbridled loyalty to Kylie, still refuse to make any comment on the artist's life beyond the standard 'Kylie's always been a nice girl'. Alternatively, many key players in Kylie's early career – some long forgotten by Kylie and Blamey – have spoken here for the first time. Several have asked that their names not be disclosed. No one was paid an interview fee.

There were a couple of other obstacles to negotiate along the Kylie research trail, many of them thrown in the way by Blamey. For instance, he faxed Mushroom Records in Melbourne, the label that originally signed Kylie, and ordered employees not to give this project any assistance.

At other points on the path, it was like triggering traps that were set in ancient times. The principal at Kylie's old high school, for example, passed on the message that no information about their famous former pupil or her less famous sibling could be released without signed authorisation from Mr Ron Minogue, who had coaxed the agreement out of the school while little Dannii was still doing maths homework.

So no Kylie in *Kylie*. But hopefully much truth.

If there's a lesson to be taken from this tale, it is best articulated by Kylie herself in the foreword to her first biography, a 32-page picture book released at the end of 1987: 'If I had to choose a moral for the story, it would be "Try hard and you can achieve anything!!" '

Hear, hear.

For now, enjoy *Kylie*!

'HI, I'M KYLIE.'

'KYLIE'

meeting the chameleon

Kylie Ann Minogue is standing here, offering a hand and a diminutive smile.

God, she's so tiny. Anyone who's ever met Kylie makes a point of telling you that but it's still a shock.

Kylie's fifteen minutes early and she's arrived alone. It's broad daylight out there and she's walked in off the street unescorted. Being one of the world's most famous pop stars, you'd expect at least a couple of sunglassed goons to be glued to her back.

You stare into that famous face and the vision blurs. There's a rush of a thousand Kylie images. You instantly try to pin them all on this redhead who's introducing herself with the practised demureness of Princess Di, but they don't quite fit.

Maybe it's the new red hair-do that's so disorientating, because all the other trademark Kylie features are present – the disproportionately large cheekbones and teeth, the crystal-clear blue eyes, the acrobatic right eyebrow that has long been 2-D Kylie's favourite tool of seduction. But with no make-up, no studio lights, this petite woman comes across as being plain and pretty rather than *Vogue* material.

It's not until Kylie pulls her hair back and momentarily freezes in profile, that eyebrow suspended way up her forehead – just like it would be in one of her music videos – that doubts about this incarnation's power finally dissolve.

This is Street Kylie (the opposite to Superstar Kylie), dressed to move among we mortals without causing the slightest flutter. Friends describe Kylie as a master of disguise. Once she used to wear wigs and dresses that would hide her distinctive form when out in public. But she's grown out of that.

Camouflaged in a tight red T-shirt and a tartan second-hand school dress, she seems to have blended unnoticed into this grungy environment. Kylie says the new red hair has given her anonymity for a week – even her grandmother didn't recognise her at first. More immediate proof is that there are at least half a dozen other people in this cafe and not one has whispered 'Is that Kylie?'

It's early afternoon, a warm day on Bondi Beach, in Sydney, late March 1995.

Kylie's back home in Australia for a holiday. Having left behind the English winter and her apartment in London for a few months, she's relaxing here following the release late last year of *Kylie Minogue*, her fifth studio album.

Although Kylie grew up in Melbourne, 1000 kilometres south of Sydney, she knows this part of the world quite well. Jason Donovan lives a short walk from this cafe. So does her boyfriend of the moment, a local actor and model named Mark Gerber. A few years ago, this city provided the setting for the initial heady days of her relationship with rock star Michael Hutchence.

These days, it seems that Kylie likes to spend more of her time playing, just having fun. Many blame the relative commercial failure of her latest album on her lack of interest in getting out and selling it. (*Kylie Minogue* only sold about half a million copies worldwide. Kylie's first album, 1988's *Kylie*, sold over five million.) But Kylie just couldn't be stuffed. The singer used to spend up to a year travelling the world pushing a new record – it was all she was doing with her life. Despite *Kylie Minogue* being her first proper full recording since 1990's *Rhythm of Love*, Kylie only spent a month on the promotional trail before setting sail for Sydney to have a rest.

That said, Kylie's had a spurt of energy since arriving back in Australia three months ago. Early into her trip, on New Year's Eve, Kylie gave an hour-long performance to two thousand ravers in a small Sydney nightclub. A few weeks later, she took a day to record a song with Nick Cave, and she took a week to make a short film, *Hayride to Hell*. For Kylie, that's the busiest things have been in a while.

Kylie has given a precious ninety minutes of her time to come into this cafe and do a bit more work. It's her only press interview of the visit, and it's for a high-brow local magazine called *The Independent Monthly*. These days, considered media positioning is what it's all about for the image of Kylie.

Kylie used to do scores of interviews a week, every week, and her answers to questions wouldn't vary much from scripted replies. It wasn't much fun for Kylie, constantly defending her popularity and combating attacks on her credibility as a performer, but it turned her into a confident and savvy media operator.

Kylie now sits there and tells you that her life would have been so much easier if she'd never granted an interview in her life, and she's never really herself in interviews anyway. So it's no surprise that personal audiences with her are such a rare media commodity. When they do happen, it's Kylie who dictates the shape they take, what will be projected.

Relaxed, chatty, funny, Kylie gives good interview. You can ask her anything, keeping in mind that she's already been asked everything, and she doesn't flinch. But she rarely lets her guard down either, never reveals too much. Any contentious points or specifics about her private life are deflected with the rhetorical flair of a statesman. Not that she's forced to ad-lib much. Most questions usually centre around her fame or current love interest,

3

subjects to which she'll cheerfully supply superficial stock-in-trade replies.

Kylie in interview has always been a well-rehearsed act. It goes some way to explaining why the young woman sitting here now is so remarkably different to the one that appeared on television last night. That was Television Kylie, fulfilling her only other media engagement of this trip, as celebrity co-host on a live variety and chat show called *Denton*. That Kylie spoke with a thick transatlantic accent as opposed to the more natural Australian inflection of today's voice.

It was a particularly cautious Kylie on TV last night, happy to play it as a prop rather than a participant, politely refusing to be drawn into any of the gags of which she obviously hadn't been forewarned. She even silently endured the teasing from one of the show's other guests, Slash from Guns N' Roses, who persisted in comparing the limousine waiting outside for Kylie to his own band's mini-van. Kylie just grinned.

'The funny thing with Slash is that he was gorgeous back-stage,' explains Interview Kylie. 'Absolutely gorgeous. I don't know whether it's the persona or the nerves or what, but he seemed quite different in the interview situation.' She pauses and looks up at the ceiling, flashes one of those multi-million dollar smiles. 'But me of all people shouldn't be saying that with an iota of surprise.

'It's just a good thing that acting is my profession,' she adds a little later, 'because I'd probably drive everybody mad. All day, every day, I'm possessed by various characters. I have a load of them.' Kylie stops herself again, lets out a laugh. 'People don't know about them and they probably won't. But, yeah. Do you know what I mean? It's a good form of release, through acting and through performing in all the different ways that I do. I think it's best for everyone that I do it. Or I would be ...' There's a flourish of hands. For an instant, Kylie is possessed by Sophia Loren. 'Oh, I don't know what I'd be.

'It would appear to me that everyone has different faces for different occasions: if you're with your family or if you're out with your crowd or if you're in a business situation. Maybe in my case it's just a bit heightened, a bit exaggerated, because so many people are looking at me so much of the time. Or trying to look *in* me. I wouldn't like to be an outsider trying to figure me out. That's why a lot of times they tend to simplify me because it makes me easier to comprehend. Or even I do sometimes. It makes it a lot easier.

'Then there's a whole other level that people don't know about. I'm willing to give so much but I think it's kind of edited, to be able to stay in control of it all, keep things together.'

With that, Interview Kylie glances at the clock on the wall. The allotted time is nearly up and she suggests there's only time for one more question.

When Kylie first walked into this cafe, no one recognised her. But for the last hour the place has been abuzz. Suddenly everyone, realising Kylie is about to walk out of their lives and back into the video screen forever, wants to have their moment with the media superstar, something they can tell their grandkids about.

The waiter passes Kylie a note. He's almost blushing. The note reads 'Ms Minogue, look over your left shoulder.' She does and a group of lads crumple into giggles. Another man, who has been obsessively watching Kylie from the next table, takes advantage of a break in conversation.

'I want a quick word before you go,' he spits out in a cockney accent.

Kylie looks over at him, smiles. 'Make it now because I'm going in five minutes.'

Man: 'I want to ask you about the acting scene here but I'll wait until you're finished.'

Kylie: 'I'm going to make a run for it, but you know, I don't know how much advice I could give you because I don't live here and I'm not too sure about where you would start.'

Man: 'I just wanted to connect with you. That's all.'

Kylie: 'Okay. Well, all the best.'

Last question. What do you think of what's happening to Jason now, Kylie? There's an extended silence. 'That's a very broad question,' answers Kylie without a smile.

Some weeks earlier, Kylie spent a few days hanging out with Jason Donovan at his waterside apartment here on Bondi Beach. It was the first time in years that the two were in each other's company for any length of time.

'It was the first opportunity to sit down and say, "Right, what the fuck's going on? How are you?"' Jason said of their recent reunion. 'I see her maybe twice a year. We catch up, gossip, compare notes. Basically, Kylie's a nice girl from the Melbourne suburbs. Then Hutchence did the makeover and there she was selling herself with this slutty image, which is so weird to me because I know her and that's not her at all.'

Obviously Donovan didn't know Kylie as well as he thought. And it's just as obvious that he still holds a lot of resentment about the way she ended things. It caught him completely off-guard, exposing his naivety and vulnerabilities. Many of those closest to Jason believe that he never recovered from Kylie, that he still loves her to this day.

It hasn't been the best of times for Jason lately. When he collapsed at the Viper Room in LA in January 1995, during supermodel Kate Moss's twenty-first birthday party – which was also attended by Michael Hutchence – it made the front pages of newspapers in Australia and the UK.

The media gleefully noted that it was the same club where, a couple of years earlier, actor River Phoenix collapsed and died.

And Jason, it turned out, was beginning to make a habit of fainting in public places. This was the third occasion in the past year.

'It was a publicity stunt,' Jason later joked. 'God, sometimes you faint, you pass out. It can happen anywhere. I'm a normal 26-year-old, I have a normal good time going out. If I happen to fall over or crash my car, then more attention is going to be laid on me than someone else.'

From Kylie's reaction, though, you can tell she doesn't approve. She takes another few seconds to consider her reply and then goes for a joke. 'I don't really know what Jason thinks about what he's doing,' she offers, laughing.

At another time, Kylie would explain how, 'I love Jason very much but there's not a lot you can say to him. Obviously friends are concerned. Jason knows I'm concerned that he's passed out a couple of times but you can't push it too far. Jason will have a way of coping.'

But here in this cafe, just for a fleeting moment, only weeks after renewing one of the closest relationships of her life, and still coming to terms with what has become of Jason, Kylie does not have a lot to say about her old boyfriend.

'I know he's a pretty easygoing guy and he'll make the best of whatever situation he's in,' she slowly continues. 'I think he's had a rough time. He's run into a bit of trouble. But maybe he likes trouble.' Another laugh. Having cracked a better joke, Kylie relaxes again.

'The thing about Jason is, he's actually quite eccentric. It's a shame people don't know more about him because he's very funny. I lost contact with him for a few years and now when I see him, I'm really pleased that he's come into his own. It's like, "You're a fruitcake, man!" But the public never see that side of him. Whether they will or not, I don't know. It's just like there's a lot of me that they don't know about or can't imagine.'

According to Jason, that's exactly the problem. Like Kylie, Jason Donovan spent his youth projecting someone else's vision of Jason Donovan.

'Now I think I've got the experience to make a few decisions myself and make a few mistakes, which I wasn't allowed before,' he explained recently. 'I just needed to take the time out to make these mistakes, to be honest.'

Indeed, the concept of honesty is a strange one when applied to the Kylie and Jason story. After all, for the four years of their love affair, the pair repeatedly swore to the world that nothing was going on. In fact, they misled us about nearly everything.

MINOGUE (JONES) –

To Carol and Ron –
a darling daughter (Kylie),
at Bethlehem, May 28

Melbourne, Australia

IT'S MID-1978 AND TEN-YEAR-OLD KYLIE

ANN MINOGUE WALKS ALONG THE CITY

STREETS OF MELBOURNE WITH HER

MOTHER, CAROL, AND YOUNGER SIBLINGS,

BROTHER BRENDAN AND SISTER DANIELLE.

LIVE AND LEARN

kylie as a child

Kylie's senses are on fire, her life altered forever.

Moments ago, Kylie witnessed the most incredible spectacle of her young life. *Grease* is the word. There's a scene towards the end of the film that leaves a lasting impression. It's where the drama's meek heroine, Sandy, played by Olivia Newton-John, drops her virginal act and struts into the House of Fun with the leather-clad bad-boy Zuko, played by John Travolta. They sing 'You're the One that I Want'.

In the years that follow, Kylie sees this three minutes of footage repeated hundreds of times on her favourite television music shows. Like every other child her age living in Western civilisation at the time, Kylie would mimic Sandy's actions in the schoolyard and in her bedroom. If little Kylie could be anyone in the world when she grew up, she wanted to be just like Sandy.

'I remember that *Grease* inspired me like nothing else,' a teenage Kylie would later admit. 'I was a prime target when *Grease* came out, so I really thought Olivia Newton-John was just, you know ... All the girls thought she was wonderful and fantastic. I was ten so subconsciously that may have had an effect. I used to think that Olivia Newton-John was amazing, like everyone else my age did at the time. I mean, everyone who saw *Grease* would have wanted to do something like that.'

Kylie Ann Minogue was born in Melbourne on 28 May 1968, four years after her parents, Carol and Ron, married and moved south from the quiet coastal town of Townsville, Queensland. Two years later, Brendan came into the family. Another year on, Danielle arrived.

Having shifted several times around Melbourne, it wasn't until Kylie's first year in high school, 1980, that the Minogues finally settled into a spacious brick home in the quiet Melbourne suburb of Surrey Hills. It was ideal – there was a large yard, schools nearby (Kylie would attend Camberwell High School), and each kid got their own room. Ron scored an accounting job with the local council and the Minogues were now living the Australian dream. They could have been one of the central families in *Neighbours*. Even their street looked like Ramsay Street.

At first, the twelve-year-old Kylie hated this new world. Her parents had once again taken her away from all her friends. But things weren't all bad. In 1979 Kylie had become an actress and quickly grew to love the profession. The opportunity came about quite by chance, thanks mainly to her little sister's innate lust for performing, even at the age of nine.

Dannii wanted Carol to take her to an audition. It was for the role of a Dutch girl called Carla on one of the most popular Australian television soaps of the 1970s, *The Sullivans*, which was set in World War Two. Carla was a war orphan who befriended a group of Australian troops. After a few episodes, she was killed off.

Dannii had been told about the role by her actress auntie, Suzette. Dannii convinced Carol to take her along, and Carol suggested that Kylie should come too. As they stepped into the studio, the casting director saw Kylie and made her Carla. Dannii was devastated.

'Mum was really good to me at the time,' the teenage Dannii

would later recall. 'She explained that Kylie was older and had more experience, that I should learn from that and enjoy the fact that she got the part.'

Kylie's main recollection of her performance years afterwards was that: 'I had to speak in a Dutch accent, which I wasn't very good at.' Dannii would eventually get her head on TV in the same show, making a brief appearance as a girl who appears to one of the soldiers back in Australia and claims to be Carla. The role required a Kylie lookalike.

The *Sullivans* gig led straight into another job for Kylie, playing a whining little girl called Robin in an episode of the airport-melodrama, *Skyways*. That's where she met Jason for the first time. Then work dried up. Once Kylie had made some new friends at school, she didn't give it a second thought. But then, a couple of years later, something terrible happened.

13

Dannii scored a spot on a weekly variety television show called *Young Talent Time. Young Talent Time* was a very popular show. The now eleven-year-old Dannii became an instant household name across Australia. Kylie almost disappeared in the dust of her little sister's fame.

Kylie was soon forced to forge Dannii's handwriting when she helped her to personally answer the constant fan mail. When Kylie now introduced herself to someone, she found it necessary to add: 'I'm Dannii's sister – from *Young Talent Time.*' It became ingrained in Kylie – maybe because everybody introduced her as such.

'I didn't like that but it was certainly no fault of Danielle's that I was introduced as her sister,' Kylie later explained. 'I never held that against her in any way.'

But it gave Kylie an inferiority complex. It was only on reaching adolescence that Kylie found an alternative to weeping. And that was sex.

In the years to follow, Kylie hardly ever mentioned this period of her life. 'I did go through one bad patch when I was about sixteen,' she revealed to a journalist one time. 'That was the terror age. I discovered boys and everything that goes with boys and I realised you didn't have to go to school. You could just wag and smoke cigarettes all day. I wasn't really bad – I just did the normal type of things.'

According to a close friend at Camberwell High, Kylie lost her virginity in a schoolroom cupboard, to one of her classmates. But that was just the start of it. Kylie and her closest girlfriends quickly developed something of a reputation with the boys around the local hang-outs in Camberwell – the swimming pools and the bowling alley.

'She was a bit of a knockabout,' said a guy called Matt who first met the young Kylie at the Camberwell Golden Bowl Centre and went on to date her on and off until the end of high school. 'I remember one night she was really drunk and she bailed me up in the toilet and started giving me a hard time and I said, "No, you're too drunk – I can't do it." I was being a nice guy.'

Kylie and Matt's dates included regularly hanging out at the local McDonald's after school and going together to mutual friend's parties on weekends. 'She was just a normal girl. She didn't do anything that anyone else didn't do. She was pretty shy but once you got to know her, once she was with friends, she was just like everyone else.'

Another guy named Paul recalled a more intimate encounter with the sixteen-year-old Kylie at a high school party in August 1984. He remembered Kylie and three other girls coming into the house. Kylie silently sat on a sofa and let a circle of boys form around her. Paul moved over and sat on the armrest and moments later was pushed into Kylie's lap. 'And I looked around – and I don't know if I said anything – but my face was suddenly right next to Kylie's face. And the next thing I know, I'm kissing her.'

Paul was a couple of years older than Kylie, having recently turned eighteen. 'We kept kissing for a while,' he continued. 'And I said to Kylie, "Look, do you want to go somewhere more private?" ' So we've got up and gone into the backyard.'

According to Paul, he then found a little cellar door leading under the house, and the pair went in and had sex. Moments later, the party came crashing through the door and Kylie immediately burst into tears, shouting, 'You used me! You used me!'

Paul promised to take her out on a date and the next week they went to see a film together. It was Kylie's favourite film, *Purple Rain*.

'It was really funny because we got off the tram and we were walking through the city and I felt like I was taking my little sister out, because she was so small. I'm walking through the city with my arm around this girl and I just felt like people were looking at me going, "He's taking out a twelve-year-old", because she didn't look sixteen.

'She was saying things like, "Oh, I can't wait to introduce you to all my friends." I must have been coming across as really cold. I've thought, I'm not going to be able to break this one off easy, which is what I really wanted to do. I came out with something like, "Oh, look, I'm coming up to my tests and it's going to be really tough for me to be seeing anyone and going out." She actually took it really well. It was almost like a change of heart. She was like, "Okay, then. That's fine. I understand that." '

For the brief time that it lasted, Kylie's sexual adventures seemed like the actions of an alter ego. To the rest of the world, even to the Minogue household, such a wild side to Kylie simply didn't exist. The details of the period went up in ashes when Kylie burned all her teenage diaries as soon as fame made its presence felt.

Once Kylie started work on *The Henderson Kids*, late in 1984, she lost interest in school. Not that she was ever a great academic.

15

'I wasn't really clever but I wasn't stupid,' offered an older Kylie. 'And I was reasonably well behaved. My best friend was a bit of a rascal but I was usually too scared to do anything naughty.'

'Even at primary school, I was more of a homey, crafty person. I'd rather sit and do something like sewing, even if it might be monotonous to someone else. I liked reading rather than, say, going out and playing netball. I wasn't sporty because with my little legs, I couldn't run very fast.'

Even after a constant run of acting jobs in 1985, Ron Minogue constantly reminded his girl not to lose her head. She had to pass Year Twelve, the final year of high school, and give herself something to fall back on. Kylie thought she'd make a great secretary because she loved organising things. Then it was a fashion course. Her dream, she regularly revealed, was to open her own handicrafts store: 'Selling things like scented drawer liners, essential oils, country gardening books, all sorts of knickknacks.'

Kylie obediently saw out her final year of school and passed well. Dannii would leave by the end of Year Ten. Brother Brendan would go on to become a TV cameraman, just like his uncle, Noel.

By the end of the school year, Kylie had come out of her shell enough to prance in front of a school assembly wearing only suspenders and a miniature uniform. Kylie and her best friend had volunteered to auction themselves off to raise money for the school ball. The value of the winning bid has been lost to history.

A matter of weeks after she sat her final exam, at the end of 1985, Kylie became Charlene.

'I always assumed I'd leave school and get a proper job,' Kylie later said. 'Then get married, have kids and look after my family in a modest little house.' Well, that vision was way off the mark.

It's early December, 1984, and a sixteen-year-old, red-headed Kylie, dressed in bright orange pants and a sleeveless floral T-shirt, is on location in country Victoria for a television mini-series called *The Henderson Kids*.

Kylie has been working on the show for two months playing Charlotte Kernow, a rough, brattish working-class kid. It's Kylie's first serious acting role, and today she loses her media virginity and gives her first interview. 'We've all cracked up at least once,' she tells a reporter from a local newspaper, describing the bond which has built up between the cast of child actors. 'We're all dreading the show finishing at the end of March. I mean, seven and a half months is practically a lifetime. What are we going to do when it ends?'

Prophetically, the reporter started her piece by explaining that: 'Kylie Minogue, 16, and [co-star] Nadine Garner, 14, would like   17
to be stars. "We're going into business together when we get older. We're going to be singers," they say.'

The only other quote attributed to Kylie is a complaint about being forced to constantly chew gum. 'I'm so sick of it,' she says, 'but it's part of my character.'

Kylie had won the part of Char earlier in the year when she, along with one thousand others, had answered a newspaper advertisement asking for would-be actors between the ages of eleven and sixteen to audition for the nine roles available in a new children's serial.

The program's producer, Alan Hardy, distinctly recalled Kylie arriving for her audition. He'd met her a few years earlier when Kylie played a small role on another program he'd worked on, *The Sullivans*. 'When Kylie came to audition, I didn't recognise her,' said Hardy. 'She'd changed so much from four years before. She was tiny, but with a grown-up face. It took me a while to realise this was the same girl that had been in *The Sullivans*.

'She came to the audition and she'd gone to a bit of trouble. She was dressed in a sort of slightly tarted-up way, in character. I can remember talking to her before the audition to try and relax her. So I asked her what she'd done. And she told me her younger sister was in *Young Talent Time* and I said, "Oh, what's that like?" And I'll never forget this. She said, "Oh, it's a bit hard having a famous sister in the family. It's a bit tough at school." And we joked about how, "Oh, one day you'll be more famous than her. Hahaha." And she did the audition and she was very good. She had a sort of edge, but [also] that lovely, cute natural thing that she has. Straightaway we just knew that she was it.'

The director of *The Henderson Kids*, Chris Langman, also clearly remembered the audition. 'She had such a high voice,' he said. 'We just cast her on a whim, really. She seemed nice. She had the sort of personality that was appealing for the part that we wanted to use her in. It was a bit of a long shot.'

But before filming could begin, a few of Kylie's natural attributes had to be altered. First, the hair. Like Kylie, Nadine Garner, the show's lead actress who would play the part of Tamara Henderson, was also a natural blonde. Hardy and Langman decided two blondes was one too many. Kylie would have to become a redhead.

'She was such a shy little kid,' said Hardy, 'and when we told her we wanted to dye her hair red, it was like the biggest trauma in her life. She was so upset. We ended up doing it and it was absolutely fine. It wasn't permanent – she used to do it in the shower every week or something. But I remember that was the biggest drama about becoming an actress – having to change her hair colour.'

The other thing which needed fixing was that voice. 'It was a bit of a struggle trying to get her to enunciate her words properly,' said Langman. 'She was sort of garbled. We did have a dialogue coach but it wasn't that bad.'

Filming of *The Henderson Kids* began in October 1984 in a variety of rural locations outside Melbourne. The $3 million production focused on the characters of Tamara Henderson and her brother Steve, played by sixteen-year-old actor Paul Smith. When the Hendersons' mother is killed in a car accident, the two are forced to move out of the city and into the care of their uncle, a policeman in a small country town. The kids have inherited land in the area and later discover there's a cave on their property with ancient Aboriginal handprints. Much of the action concerns their struggle to protect the cave from the clutches of a greedy land developer.

Kylie's character Char becomes Tamara's best friend in town. Off-screen, Kylie and Nadine Garner also built up an immediate rapport. 'Nadine was very good for Kylie,' said Hardy, 'because Nadine was more outgoing. They hit it off from day one. It was a pair.

'Kylie was very shy. Very, very shy. She had to be really encouraged. She was very uncertain, lacking in confidence. The only time she appeared totally relaxed was when she and Nadine Garner would be around the set and they would sing. Always singing. It was sensational. They'd just sit and harmonise. There were enough people around with show-business nous who were saying, "These kids have great voices." '

Kylie would later confirm how, 'It was during that time that I became more interested in singing because another girl on the set, Nadine Garner, we always used to sing together. It was the first time I remember that I harmonised.'

Garner, who would go on to become one of Australia's most respected actresses in film and television, also has fond memories of her and Kylie constantly singing together. 'We were very unexceptional kids,' said Garner. 'We were just workers. But there was a lot of joy, and music was a big part of that. We sang all the time. That was a wonderful part of our companionship, the fact that our voices sounded so beautiful together. That was great for me, to find someone who loved music as much as I did and was obsessed with it like I was.

'Our musical tastes were very different. She was right into Prince, Violent Femmes and Donna Summer. A lot of funky music, black music. I was listening to Bob Dylan and folkie stuff. I don't think my musical tastes influenced hers but I remember listening to her stuff. And singing with her. Anything. We used to spend hours and hours doing that.'

Garner perceived the young Kylie quite differently to the older members of the cast and crew on *The Henderson Kids*. 'Kylie was very ambitious,' said Garner. 'Very quietly ambitious. There was this sense of self that she had. I can't explain it. There was just something about her that was determined, I guess. Not in a way that was repellent or unfriendly. I didn't know at the time what that would bring her but she had a great sense of herself.'

Away from their respective families and sharing hotel rooms over the six-month shoot, Garner and Kylie found themselves treating each other as de facto siblings. 'She's exactly the same age as my sister,' explained Garner, 'and she's got a sister my age so we probably did a bit of role-playing in terms of that. She was an older girl who was much more worldly than I was, even at sixteen. She was kind of aware of her womanhood and her femininity, those kind of things. She was fragile too.'

Director Langman had realised just how fragile Kylie could be. 'I remember shouting at her one time and she burst into tears. It was for no reason. I think I just made a bad joke or something like that. I didn't really get to know her at all until we got near the end of it. And then it finished.'

Kylie's timidness affected her work. According to Hardy, Kylie's acting was very tentative early on and it wasn't until a scene in which her character loses her job and breaks down in tears that Kylie started becoming more confident with her craft.

The 'breakthrough scene', as Hardy called it, occurs when Char makes a mess of dyeing the land developer's wife's hair, leaving her with a green do. The distraught apprentice runs off into the bushes, where she is found in tears by Steve Henderson.

A couple of years later, Kylie recalled that same scene as a turning point in her career. 'I remember the first time I had to cry on-screen,' she said. 'I was really nervous but found out I could do it. The scene worked out really well. Now I can get to those emotional moments and I can express them.' But it would take a lot of practice over the years in *Neighbours* before she could do it convincingly.

That aside, Kylie gave a fairly commendable performance in *The Henderson Kids*, getting visibly stronger and more confident as the twelve-part series progressed. 'She's always had a natural talent,' observed Langman. 'She's just very professional as far as always being prepared, always being on time, always being focused and always being very aware of her image and her look.'

When filming wrapped up in March 1985, it proved to be a traumatic moment in the lives of the nine children involved. 'It was very, very, very emotional,' recalled Garner. 'We'd created this little microcosm of a world, and when it ended, none of us knew how to go back to the bigger picture, the big world. I didn't. I grieved for a long time. Six months when you're thirteen feels like an eternity.'

Like Kylie and Garner, most of the other young performers involved with *The Henderson Kids* would continue to pursue careers in acting. Of particular note is Ben Mendelsohn, who has become one of the country's premier film actors, and Annie Jones, who would end up starring alongside Kylie in *Neighbours*.

At the wrap party, Kylie and Garner sang together one last time in front of the cast and crew. Their friendship didn't end up surviving off the set but Garner said she cherished what they experienced together, describing it as 'very nourishing for the short time that it lasted. Intense, short, meaningful, finished'.

By the time *The Henderson Kids* went to air in Australia, on 11 May 1985, Kylie was a blonde again and had already been back at school for a couple of months. Although she'd missed the opening few weeks of her final year while filming was underway, on-set tutors had helped Kylie keep up with her studies. The tutors had also helped see the struggling student through the final exams of the previous year's studies.

'That was another thing I was really proud about Kylie,' said Hardy. 'She had to pass English to get her Year Eleven and it was her weakest subject and she was really worried about it. And our tutor did a lot of work on it with her. She worked very hard [and] it was difficult to concentrate. We were very proud that, despite all those distractions, she got the subject she needed to pass.'

The Henderson Kids was a ratings success, prompting a sequel of another twelve hour-long episodes to be put into the works. Meanwhile, Kylie's performance had indirectly helped her score a couple of roles in other shows.

Immediately following *The Henderson Kids*, Kylie guest-starred in another children's program from the same production house, Crawford's, called *The Zoo Family*. In her solitary appearance in the show, the now nearly seventeen-year-old Kylie played a twelve-year-old character named Yvonne in a half-hour episode entitled 'Yvonne the Terrible'.

A battered child, Yvonne is taken in by the family of a zoo caretaker over the school holidays. She turns out to be a nightmare, vandalising zoo property and letting animals out of their cages. It's only when she sees a battered kangaroo return to its mother that she finally starts to settle down.

'By the time of *Zoo Family*,' said the show's producer, Gwenda Marsh, 'Kylie walked on that set a full professional. You just knew she was going to be a stayer.'

In May 1985, Kylie landed another mini-series, this time beating fifty other girls for the female lead in the six-part *Fame and Misfortune*.

Playing Samantha Collins, the conniving, antagonistic sister of the show's main protagonist, Kylie proved in her limited on-air time that she was quickly maturing as an actress. 'It was clear just from the auditioning process that she was a kid that had very good instincts and a lot of natural talent,' said director and producer Noel Price. 'She was a cute little kid, a nice kid. She certainly, at that stage, still wasn't a name among child actors but she came across as a person who was very bright and had a lot of natural on-screen charm.'

Kylie's young co-star in *Fame and Misfortune*, Myles Collins, saw Kylie as a teacher while on set. She and Ben Mendelsohn, her co-star from *The Henderson Kids*, behaved like seniors to the juvenile cast, often taking it upon themselves to gee up the schoolyard extras before scenes.

Off-screen, Kylie took to the fifteen-year-old Collins as if he actually was her little brother. The two often hung around with the crew after filming for beers in the studio canteen. Kylie was loosening up around people. On weekends, the pair would sneak off into an adjoining studio at the Australian Broadcasting Corporation where Australia's longest-running music program, *Countdown*, was shot each week. Throughout Kylie's life, *Countdown* had been a weekly window onto the glamorous fantasy world of pop music. Now she was seeing it from inside, from the director's box.

In two years' time, during the height of 'Locomotion', Kylie would be given the honour of hosting the final show of the

23

thirteen-year-old program. By that stage Kylie didn't need *Count-down* anymore. She was living the real thing.

But for the moment, as filming for *Fame and Misfortune* came to an end in August 1985, Kylie's fledgling acting career was about to suffer its first setback. *The Henderson Kids II* was about to enter production and Kylie's character Char had been written out of the storyline.

'I can remember Kylie came in to look at some photos,' recalled Alan Hardy, 'and I had to sit her down and say, "There's no part for you in the second series." I was really disappointed and so was she. I explained all the reasons, but of course, it was the best thing I ever did for her.

'I feel that I made her career because, by knocking her back for a part in that, she was able to go and do *Neighbours.*'

CHARLENE MITCHELL IS BORN.

GOOD NEIGHBOURS

kylie and charlene

It's late January, 1986, and Kylie is sitting alone on a casting couch inside a small crammed office in inner-city Melbourne, staring at her own live image on a nearby television monitor. Kylie has been asked to stay put for a moment as Jan Russ, the talent director of a fledgling five-night-a-week TV drama called *Neighbours*, runs off in search of the show's producer, John Holmes.

A few minutes later, Russ returns with Holmes following. She instructs the producer to concentrate on the screen and asks Kylie to read again from the top of the page.

Suddenly, the usually timid, introverted Kylie is acting nothing like herself. Kylie's become loud, annoyingly squeaky, has at this instant acquired an open-mouthed expression which projects pure confusion back at the world. Kylie has become Charlene.

'She just looked very plain, a very mousy, shy little thing,' recalled Jan Russ of Kylie's audition. 'She had no make-up on and she just had her hair down. What she was reading had a lot of life to it. I looked at her sitting there and then suddenly saw this other image on the monitor. And I thought, my God, this kid really has something that's coming through on the screen. You could see the structure of her face and the camera really loved her – there was something happening between the two of them. So I thought, This kid's the one for this role – there's nobody else.'

Producer John Holmes agreed, if somewhat less enthusiastically.

'I don't think Kylie walked in on a big ray of sunshine or under the spotlight with us thinking, my God, we've got to have this girl!' offered Holmes. 'Kylie was one of probably forty or fifty girls we'd interviewed for the part of Charlene and she was the one that stood out. It's the sense of the producer and the casting director to pick the right people and identify the "IT" quality some of the kids have and most of them don't. So, in a way, Kylie picked herself.

'In the audition, she was bright and bubbly, very keen. And she had some lovely qualities – the girl-next-door but with some spirit. She had all the characteristics that we needed for the character of Charlene.'

Within a couple of months, on 18 April 1986, Kylie's debut appearance as Charlene Mitchell in *Neighbours* went to air in Australia. Kylie's initial thirteen-week contract for the role was quickly extended to twenty-six weeks but the actress would end up being Charlene until June 1988.

It wasn't only pre-teens who developed a daily addiction for *Neighbours.* The supporting cast of senior characters – from Charlene's nagging mother Madge (played by Anne Charleston) to Scott's disciplinary father Jim (Alan Dale) to the neighbourhood gossip Mrs Mangel (Vivean Gray) to the Robinsons' guru granny Helen (Anne Haddy) – offered a Nuremberg Rally of conservative opinion to suck in the olds. Along with a sprinkle of twenty-something characters, there was a virtual UN of cross-generational, socio-political belief reflected within the handful of households on this magical street.

By early 1988, with some two million addicts in Australia and another thirteen million in the UK, the *Neighbours* epidemic had made such a cultural impact that a heart-shaped wedding photo of Charlene and her boyfriend, Scott Robinson, landed on the cover of the Australian edition of *Time* magazine.

It seemed even *Time* had succumbed to the unbearable niceness of being *Neighbours*. It dedicated a special issue 'to all those who are in love and all those who can remember' and tried to make sense of the program's popularity. It described the phenomenon as a new era of television entertainment, 'in which the everyday has replaced melodrama . . . the focus has moved from bedswapping, wicked secrets, power plays and bitchiness to the gentle, comforting and often rustic charm of communities of nice people who are kind to each other. It is soap as social engineering.'

Australian TV critic David Lyle suggested to *Time* that *Neighbours* had already irreversibly dented the real world. 'Charlene has done more to alter people's attitudes to sex discrimination in jobs than any other single factor,' opined Lyle, adding that programs such as *Neighbours* 'take few risks, and they don't reach pinnacles of art as some other shows do. But you can't dismiss them as purely trivial when they are so popular.'

29

Most other 'serious' media commentators didn't agree. They found it much easier to write off *Neighbours* as populist crap, mocking it as 'the cheapest soap on the market' rather than offering any creative diagnosis of the product's appeal.

Neighbours' creator, Reg Watson, attributed his show's popularity to 'the fact that we let young people communicate with adults. We wrote the teenagers as adults. That was the thinking behind it. And we didn't have villains hanging around – the villain was life itself. Of course, it worked really well. There was a universal need at that point for someone to write about a small, warm community.'

For her part, Kylie regularly admitted to not having the faintest idea about what made her alter ego so charismatic: '. . . because she's an average teenager who had problems with her boyfriend and with getting a career started,' was the depth of Kylie's analysis. 'I'm a Gemini which means that I'm two people. I've got my noisy side but I also have my quiet, shy side. I don't think Charlene really has a quiet side. Charlene is really sensitive but doesn't show it. She'd rather die than be caught crying. She honestly believes she can do everything better than anyone else. But she's also a hopeless liar and gets caught out every time.

'Charlene is much more tomboyish and outspoken than what I am,' was another point the young actress regurgitated regularly. 'She will generally say what she thinks, which is a good thing.' Smile. 'She's a bit of a rebel and they probably relate to that.' Smile. 'While she has her problems, she will always come out on top.'

Did Kylie want to be more like Charlene? Sorry, no more questions now: Kylie needs her rest.

Neighbours was hardly a success story when Kylie started filming in February, 1986. Only five months earlier, the Seven network – the Australian television station which had launched *Neighbours* at a cost of $8 million in early 1985 – axed the nightly half-hour show due to poor ratings across Australia (with the notable exception of Melbourne, where *Neighbours* occasionally won its six o'clock timeslot). In an unprecedented move, an opposing TV network, Ten, immediately decided to revive the serial. But despite encouraging signs from the public, *Neighbours* was again in the queue for the chopping block when Charlene arrived in Erinsborough.

Neighbours was developed and produced by an independent television production company called Grundy Television Productions. Along with Crawford's (the production house recently responsible for *The Henderson Kids* and *The Zoo Family*), Grundy's had provided Australian television with the bulk of its local drama in recent years. Since the mid-seventies, *Neighbours*' creator and executive producer, Reg Watson, a longtime employee of Grundy's, had conceptualised some of Australian television's other most popular soaps, including *Prisoner*, *Sons and Daughters*, *The Restless Years* and *The Young Doctors*.

Watson based *Neighbours* on the gentle manner of his hometown suburb in Brisbane, Queensland. 'Up there,' according to Watson, 'they had a different attitude. There was a feeling of great community. If you went to the beach and it rained, your neighbour would run and take your washing off the line and fold it. They did things like that. It was a very warm feeling.

'At that time, we were so used to everything on TV being shock-horror and all that rubbish,' added the man previously responsible for such characters as *Prisoner*'s top dog Bea Smith and *Sons and Daughters*' Pat the Bitch. 'We got away from all that.'

Neighbours first aired on the Seven network on 18 March 1985. The show was cut soon after its original 26-week contract expired, the final episode screening in November of that year. It was then relaunched by the Ten network in a 7 p.m. timeslot on 20 January 1986.

'Ten knew what they were buying,' explained producer John Holmes, another Grundy employee who moved with *Neighbours* to its new network. 'It wasn't just a piece of paper with ideas and character breakdowns – it was actually a 26-week pilot. So Ten could see what they felt were the strengths and weaknesses of the program and they went about giving us a brief to change it. Ten had nothing to lose in those days. They had *M*A*S*H* running at seven o'clock which, by then, was on its eighth or ninth re-run.'

The main directive from the executives at Ten was for more emphasis to be placed on *Neighbours*' youth storylines. The breakdown of ratings figures from the show's last few months on Seven revealed strong viewer support among fourteen- to eighteen-year-old females. This demographic, Ten decided, was the show's prime target audience.

The Ten network's strategy for *Neighbours* had little to do with the content of the program itself. In taking the gamble of reviving a proven failure, Ten was placing all its chips on an innovative publicity campaign devised by the station's in-house promotions department. This publicity campaign could easily have been adapted for any other show.

Indeed, Reg Watson insisted that he and his team of writers didn't alter their approach towards *Neighbours* in any way to facilitate the station swap-over. 'Everyone said we changed it for Channel Ten,' said Watson, 'but that wasn't true. We just continued the same stories with a break in between.'

Ten revealed its intention to pick up *Neighbours* within days of the axe falling at Seven. One minute, producer John Holmes was addressing his cast about impending pink slips; the next, he was going around telling everyone not to make any plans to leave town.

'It was a different matter at Channel Ten,' suggested Holmes. 'At Ten, *Neighbours* was the show of the year to make work. There was a guy who was the head of promotion and publicity in those days, Brian Walsh, and he was definitely a major influence in making *Neighbours* a hit. He kind of rewrote the book on television promotion – big publicity events, crossover promotion to radio, in-store promotions in shopping centres. It was kind of like blanket bombing. Brian Walsh had an idea and he exploited it.'

Brian Walsh was as close as Kylie got to a Svengali figure in these early years. From the day *Neighbours* started on Channel Ten, cast members were put on a rigorous promotional trail that saw them flying across Australia each weekend to make personal appearances at shopping malls and nightclubs.

'We enforced a very heavy demand on all the actors for publicity, particularly the young ones,' said Brian Walsh. 'We certainly inferred that without their support, the show wasn't going to last. If the show didn't last, they wouldn't have a job.

'So right from the very start they knew they had a commitment to promote the show, probably more than any other cast member of any other show in a similar genre. But they were also well looked after. They got loads of trips away, lots of good times. These were kids who had stepped out of a school bus and into a limousine. They were going from pocket money of eight dollars a week to a pay-cheque of $2000.'

At that time, it wasn't customary for soap actors in Australia to fiercely publicise their roles. Quite the contrary – many young actors preferred to avoid it, seeing their soap work as simply a way of paying the bills until real work arrived. Back when the show was still at Seven, one former cast member, David Clencie, who played Danny Ramsay, had refused to pose for the cover of the popular weekly magazine, *TV Scene*.

33

Kylie and Jason had no such qualms. Kylie especially was just grateful for the work. As one of *Neighbours*' regular directors observed: 'The thing about Jason and Kylie, particular Kylie, was that she didn't realise how crappy the show was. And she went with it. She believed it to be the best thing that had ever happened, and ultimately it was, because she made it that way. She wasn't that discerning at her age as other people might have been. Kylie was like, "Yeah, I relate to this. I like it." She had a great attitude towards making it work.'

And so did the rest of the *Neighbours*' cast. After all, they'd already survived one demolition of their neighbourhood. And nearly everyone appreciated that it was the new kids on the block, Kylie and Jason, who were now keeping this town alive.

'Obviously, the Kylie and Jason promotion in that show was pretty much the key to its success,' stated Brian Walsh. 'Certainly it's fair to say it was an ensemble cast, so people like Guy Pearce and Elaine Smith and Peter O'Brien and, later, Craig McLachlan were all crucial to the show's success, but the press had a love affair with Kylie and Jason and Charlene and Scott.

'The first three months were fairly rocky. Indeed, the show wasn't a success at all. It wasn't until first Jason and then Kylie came into the show that it picked up. So they tend to be remembered as the two people that were responsible for *Neighbours*' success but, in fact, it was a much wider push than just those two.'

Still, Walsh pinpointed a trip to Sydney for some filming with Kylie and Jason late in 1986 as the pivotal event in transforming *Neighbours* from a popular program into an Australian television phenomenon.

'We couldn't get any coverage of *Neighbours* in Sydney,' he recalled. 'It was a diabolical problem for us because the press just refused to acknowledge the show existed, let alone was popular. One of the promotions we implemented was a huge shopping centre promotion around Sydney. The show was filmed in Melbourne so we flew the cast up every weekend and we used to take them out to shopping centres.

'It started off with fifty or sixty kids that would come and see the *Neighbours* cast. But that soon grew and, by about the end of the ninth week of doing these appearances, there were some crowds of five or six thousand people. And, at the same time, the press still didn't recognise the show's success.'

Walsh got a film crew to tape some of the 'riots'. He sent a copy to the editor of every magazine and newspaper in the country, with a note explaining that 'although the ratings don't reflect this show's popularity, here's some vision of some riots that have been taking place out at Westfield Shoppingtowns. Just goes to show you what sort of show it is and how popular it is.'

The editor of Sydney's highest-circulating tabloid, *The Daily*

Mirror, took the bait. At home, watching the video, his fifteen-year-old daughter broke the news to him that *Neighbours* was already the biggest thing in schoolyard culture since the yo-yo.

'So he decided it was the sort of show that *The Daily Mirror* in Sydney should get behind,' expanded Walsh. 'That's how it started.'

The next step was to come up with an angle for a story. Kylie and Jason were already booked in to do some filming at Manly beach in Sydney so Walsh invited his new press friends along. 'And that was when Charlene and Scott had their first on-screen kiss. From what was a fairly innocent throwaway kiss that you'd see these days in any episode of *Home and Away* or *Echo Point* [a recent, short-lived *Neighbours* clone], we certainly built it up to be the greatest screen kiss ever. And the front page of the *Daily Mirror* that afternoon came out with the headline "TV Shock – Teen Sex on TV Tonight". And it was just an innocent kiss but that gave Kylie and Jason their very first front page, gave *Neighbours* its very first front page, and that's what really started the ball rolling.

'From then, the Scott and Charlene publicity machine went into overdrive and it became a matter of control. We didn't have to fabricate or invent much. It pretty much had its own steam.'

Soon, Kylie and Jason's faces were in newspapers every other day, on the cover of the national television guide, *TV Week*, nearly every week. Kylie and Jason were now, officially, stars.

'It wasn't rocket science,' concluded Walsh, 'it was just a matter of hard work, and an extremely co-operative cast. I guess they were there when the show was going through its bad patches so they knew what sort of hard work had to be put in to get the results.'

But some dissident residents on the set of Ramsay Street still privately grumbled about all the attention that was constantly being showered on those two amateurs. 'It was always a very happy cast but there was definitely a division between the older members of the cast and the younger members,' revealed Walsh. 'And a lot of the older members certainly resented the success of Kylie and Jason.

'One particular member, who's still on the program [actress Anne Haddy, who plays grandma Helen Daniels] just used to treat the kids – as we called them – in a terrible manner. I used to see it go on all the time. She resented the fact that, as actors, they were overlooked while the children were used to promote the show. But she failed to realise what the market was saying.'

But one woman's whingeing wasn't going to spoil Kylie's party. Anyway, most of Kylie's spare time on set was spent solely in the company of Jason or with station employees that were more than happy to constantly remind the young actress that she was now a supernova.

Still, Kylie has said that three of the men in the cast – Jason of course, Ian Smith (who played Charlene's stepfather, Harold) and Alan Dale (Scott's father, Jim Robinson) – became some of her closest friends. 'They were all incredibly supportive to me,' she remarked on leaving the show. 'They were like boyfriends, brothers, fathers and uncles rolled into one.'

Kylie's work day, like everyone's on the show, would start early in the morning and not end until evening. Usually, if Kylie was staying at her parents' house for the night, she'd be up by 5.30 a.m. to catch a cab for the ten-minute ride to the Channel Ten studios in Nunawading.

By 7.30 a.m., having already sat in make-up for an hour, it was into rehearsals. For a one-minute scene, *Neighbours*' actors had a fifteen-minute run-through. It would then take another twenty minutes to film. Kylie would often have to shoot up to twenty-five separate scenes a day. Evenings at home would be spent memorising the following day's dialogue. Some nights, there'd be a helicopter waiting right on 7.30 p.m. to dash the stars to a public engagement.

'The thing that I remember so much about Kylie was she was always there,' said one of the show's many regular directors, Andrew Friedman. 'She was always aware of her work. Some other kids, or actors, would come in and they'd be there for half the time or their minds were somewhere else.

'But the thing about Kylie, even at the height of her career with the music and the publicity, she was always there. Always early, always keen and always wanting to learn. Some of the others, they didn't even sometimes turn up. Kylie was so professional in terms of her work.'

Neighbours first appeared on British television at midday on 26 October 1986. Charlene and Scott didn't come into the picture until the middle of the following year. On the first day of January 1988, the BBC – bowing to fan-mail pressure and complaints that having *Neighbours* on at midday was causing havoc with truancy levels at schools across the UK – took the radical step of replaying each day's episode at 5.30 p.m., immediately prior to the station's main evening news bulletin. By the middle of 1988, estimates had *Neighbours* drawing between fifteen and twenty million British viewers a night – more people than the whole population of Australia. During the Gulf War, *Neighbours* was the only show on the BBC not to be interrupted.

'I never had any doubts as to whether Britain would like *Neighbours*,' chuckled creator Reg Watson. 'When the BBC came over here, I said it would work in Britain if you give it the right time slot.'

Watson had spent nearly a decade in the UK producing the popular television serial *Crossroads*. 'So I knew what they would like and what they wouldn't like. You've got to remember that in

Britain, there was no publicity at all and *Neighbours* went through the roof.'

By the time Kylie quit the show in June 1988, *Neighbours* was being seen in forty-five countries around the world. The success of Kylie's 'Locomotion', compounded by the hype surrounding Charlene and Scott's wedding, saw *Neighbours'* popularity hit hysteria levels in Australia by mid-1987. It would take the lagging UK a few months and the release of 'I Should Be So Lucky' for the program to peak there.

The invasion of Britain caused the instant assault of Australia by the hounds of Fleet Street. Even though local media coverage of Kylie and Jason had hit unprecedented, fanatical proportions, Australia had never before witnessed the zealous, no-holds-barred reporting style of the English press.

The British obsession with Kylie began in earnest in Sydney on 26 January 1988, the day of Australia's Bicentennial celebrations, in the mad scramble by media crews to photograph Princess Diana shaking hands with the new princess of the little screen. Within two weeks, 'Lucky' was on top of the charts in the UK and Kylie, like other royals before her, quickly had to learn to adapt to a life surrounded by obtrusive shadows carrying cameras.

Everyone was now in search of whatever dirt they could get on this holier-than-thou Kylie/Charlene. In sterling British tabloid tradition, there was a rush to expose any mud that might lie under the angel dust. And what better target than the star of a show with such high moral fibre?

Neighbours' producers went out of their way to deliver two and a half hours of wholesome family entertainment a week that was guaranteed not to offend anyone. Contentious storylines were always meticulously scrubbed. When Charlene and Scott first broached the idea of moving in together, conservative fans in

Australia went into an uproar. Early in Kylie's tenure, a whole afternoon's filming was scrapped when its subject matter – Charlene discussing the pill with her mum – failed to pass the show's self-imposed censorship standards.

By this stage, Kylie and Jason couldn't step on to a city street without being besieged by media. Pin Oak Court, the location that acted as Ramsay Street, was put under 24-hour security surveillance. One entrepreneur started up tourist bus trips to the site. That venture came to an abrupt end when actor Alan Dale got into an argument with the guy over distribution of profits and punched him out.

Soon, everyone was making money out of *Neighbours*. A board game of the show became a bestseller. There were countless authorised and unauthorised publications and tonnes of merchandise being pumped out of printers. All the actors were drawing huge appearance fees. Some chose to drop out of the show and grab the huge money being offered by the English pantomime circuit.

Of course, Kylie knew exactly where her next few millions were coming from.

Kylie filmed her last scene of *Neighbours* on 10 June 1988. The show's producers had realised months earlier that it was inevitable they would soon lose their star. 'She knew her priority was to *Neighbours*,' said Brian Walsh. 'In the end, that was the reason she gave it up because she couldn't do it justice. And she'd burned out. She could only do so many more interviews as Charlene and she'd reached her peak and it was time to move on. There was a good six months where she was burning the candle at both ends and she just exhausted herself.

'Kylie quite regularly complained of overexhaustion but she brought it on herself. I don't mean that in an unfair way, but in her pursuit of success as both a performer and an actor, she had to balance two careers. It was pretty daunting and that's what really knocked her about. She had a lot of people putting a lot of pressure on her success: the network, the producers, her manager, her parents, her record company. All those people putting in all that energy so that one person could pop out success after success. It's no wonder she burned out after a while.'

Still, *Neighbours'* producers weren't going to let Kylie go without one last shot at holding on. One afternoon after she'd tendered her resignation, the show's hierarchy took Kylie out for a quiet lunch away from the star's possessive manager and father. 'We wanted to have a talk to Kylie and try to talk her out of it,' admitted casting director Jan Russ. 'But we didn't. Kylie said that, no, she'd made up her mind and she really wanted to leave and go on to other things.'

Ironically, the producers probably would have got some support out of Mr Minogue. The accountant still wasn't convinced his daughter was making the right move. After all, *Neighbours* delivered a hefty pay cheque without fail every week. Meanwhile, this rock'n'roll game, for all its talk of number ones and international acclaim, still hadn't coughed up a single cent into the Minogue trust.

Of course, all this didn't matter now – the decision was made. Kylie's last scene was Charlene's farewell, the character waving goodbye as her car headed back home to Queensland. Charlene's grandfather had given her a house. Despite recent matrimonial disharmony, Scott intended soon to follow.

Both on- and off-screen, Kylie couldn't control the tears that afternoon. 'I thought my last day was going to be emotional and it was,' the actress admitted later. 'I bawled my eyes out.'

That evening, there was a 'secret' party in Kylie's honour at a restaurant in Melbourne. The cast and crew presented Kylie with an antique dresser mirror and a farewell card made up of a montage of all her smiley promotional photos. Although Kylie was taken in and out of the celebrations via a back entrance, she couldn't escape the press. 'It's been a really sad day,' Kylie told them on leaving the restaurant at 1 a.m. en route to a city nightclub. 'I'll be sorry to leave the show.'

Inside the restaurant, the overwhelmed Kylie had burst into tears three times as she stood up to give thanks. She asked the hundred friends and crew not to look at her. With her hands over her face, muttering that, 'If I don't look at you I won't cry,' Kylie thanked everyone for their 'support over the years'.

'I don't think anyone understood a word I said through all the sniffling and mumbling,' Kylie would add a few days later. 'I really will miss the cast members.

'I cried because I knew when I walked out on Ramsay Street, it would be a hundred times more difficult to see my friends. At the moment, I am just flowing with the tide, following whatever is on offer to me that I like. There is obviously an ambitious streak in me but I do realise that I am still very young and inexperienced. I have never written a song or acted in theatre or a big movie, so there is still lots to learn.

'As for *Neighbours*, there is always the possibility I could go back to it, the door has been left open for Charlene to reappear at any time. There is no way I would support those who degrade it. *Neighbours* projects being honest and always has a happy ending. We are not in an ideal world and so I guess it is like a fantasy to them [the audience]. Everything is spelt out, it's like getting it on a silver platter, so they can go off for half an hour and get lost in this pretend world.

'I owe a hell of a lot to *Neighbours* and I will always remember that. Okay, so it isn't *Gone with the Wind*, but it's popular, very popular, and I'm proud to have been associated with it.'

Regardless of these words, in a little over a year, Kylie's agents were in court trying to legally kill off Charlene and any traces of their superstar's link to the low-budget soap.

The planned commercial release of a ninety-minute video compilation entitled *Scott and Charlene: A Love Story* in the middle of 1989 infuriated Kylie and her people. Put out by *Neighbours'* production house, Grundy's, the video featured edited highlights of Kylie's scenes with Jason from the series.

Kylie tried to stop its release. Her lawyers argued that Kylie's career would be 'significantly and adversely affected' by the video, forever typecasting the entertainer as Charlene and, in turn, preventing Kylie from generating a wider and older audience. They added that Kylie had been 'at pains to develop a career as a sophisticated singer' and had spent considerable 'time, money and effort' in ridding herself of Charlene.

The presiding judge, who confessed he'd never heard of Kylie Minogue before the case and that he'd fast-forwarded his way through the video because he 'wasn't prepared to spend an hour and a half to watch it', ruled in favour of Grundy's. He found that Kylie's case was fundamentally weak considering how obvious it was to everyone that the success of *Neighbours* had directly launched her career.

Kylie didn't accept the judgement quietly. 'I was trying to set a precedent for all actors in Australia,' she said in interviews. 'Grundy's, by asking my permission [to release the video], accepted that they had to get permission, and then when I didn't give it, they went ahead and did it anyway and then held it against me in court that I hadn't seen the video.

'I was contracted to appear on the *Neighbours* series each night, and now what they've done is turn it into a completely new package. It's not even *Neighbours*. That's not what I was paid a measly fee of money for. It's Grundy's that are making money out of it, not me. But the money is not the principle.

'I have spent a lot of time getting away from Charlene,' further bristled Kylie, adding that she wouldn't even think about tuning in to watch the show anymore. 'I don't want this sort of thing stuck on the shelves forever. I'm sure there are a lot of people who say, "*Neighbours* made you what you are". Well, it hasn't. It's exploitation.'

Kylie's last scene as Mrs Charlene Mitchell Robinson went to air on British television on 31 October 1989. (In 1996, a cable station was still broadcasting re-runs of the Charlene and Scott series on weekday afternoons.) Within a year of Kylie's departure, *Neighbours* lost the majority of its original high-profile young stars.

The events in Ramsay Street never again hit the same peaks of popularity, but the neighbourhood survived the loss of Charlene. Still in production a decade after Kylie's debut, *Neighbours* has seen its cast regenerate several times over. In 1996, new episodes of the decade-old show were still drawing a respectable eleven million viewers a day in the UK.

43

FILMED IN MELBOURNE, *NEIGHBOURS* – A NIGHTLY HALF-HOUR SOAP OPERA THAT RELAYED THE PEDESTRIAN LIVES OF THE RESIDENTS OF RAMSAY STREET, IN THE SUBURB OF ERINSBOROUGH – WAS ALREADY SHOWING AN UPTURN IN RATINGS IN SEVERAL AUSTRALIAN CITIES BY THE TIME THE SEVENTEEN-YEAR-OLD KYLIE ARRIVED TO FILM HER FIRST SCENES AS CHARLENE MITCHELL.

ESPECIALLY FOR YOU

kylie and jason,
charlene and scott

Fatally close to being axed only a month earlier, the program was saved by an expanding audience of Australian schoolgirls that had apparently developed an insatiable infatuation with the all-Australian Scott Robinson.

Written in as a mate for Scott, Charlene's stay was supposed to be a brief one, only thirteen weeks. But it was immediately obvious to everyone that something oddly special was happening. The weekly TV rating sheets were proving it.

Kylie and Jason had met once before, on the set of another Australian soap, *Skyways*, six years earlier. The two played brother and sister. Kylie's only recollection of those few days together as kids was that Jason was 'really chubby with a bowl haircut and I was really small with straight blonde hair'.

Quite a different human being was waiting for Kylie when she stepped into the *Neighbours* backstage caravan before shooting that first scene. Tall, muscular and handsome, the now seventeen-year-old Jason Donovan had grown into the type of boyfriend that Kylie, like most other suburban schoolgirls, fantasised about.

Kylie recognised Jason the moment she laid eyes on him. In an outward burst of emotion that belied her usually timid persona around strangers, Kylie greeted Jason like this was the greatest reunion of her life. 'You remember, don't you?' she said. It only took a second for the joy to disappear from Kylie's face. In its place fell that look of annoyance that would soon become a Charlene trademark. Jason didn't have a clue who she was.

Kylie composed herself and reminded him. Jason took a moment longer to superimpose the face of that little girl he'd had the briefest crush on a lifetime ago to this young woman who was now looking at him as if she was about to burst into tears. Then Jason remembered.

Within no time, the two novice actors were lovers, had sworn everlasting devotion to each other. In the times to come, the conviction of Kylie and Jason's hastily exchanged vows would be strenuously tested.

Kylie and Jason couldn't get over how happy they were in those first couple of months together. Everything suggested they were ideally suited. Like, the chances of them being on TV together all those years ago and then meeting again like this. Like, they were both Geminis, and born only four days apart. Cosmic. It was obvious that fate had played a hand in their fairytale.

As she had done with previous boyfriends, Kylie immediately submerged herself into Jason's existence. He became everything to her, her world. As far as Kylie was concerned, she had met the man who would be her husband, the father of her children. Things couldn't have been better for Jason either. He quickly realised that Kylie was a much different person when away from crowds, dropping that mousy act she'd play when others were around.

Now that they were togther forever, they needed nothing and no one. Anyway, Kylie and Jason already felt like they had everything. They both had their dream jobs. They were rich, earning $2000 a week – heaps of money considering they were high-school students only weeks before they started on *Neighbours*. They were even getting stopped in the streets and asked for autographs, just like famous actors. On top of all that, they got to hug and kiss while working, right there in front of the cameras.

But then one afternoon, only a couple of months into their relationship, Kylie and Jason's blind bliss got a spray of acidic reality. The poison was administered innocently enough.

It came without warning one day in mid-1986 when a TV executive asked to have a quiet word to the two teenagers while they were hanging around the set. The man was Brian Walsh, the promotions manager for Channel Ten, the station broadcasting *Neighbours* in Australia. Walsh was responsible for devising the innovative publicity campaign that was currently propelling the show's ratings skywards, and he quickly realised early in the piece that Kylie and Jason were creating magic on the small screen. He'd also got to know the kids personally during their numerous promotional trips around Australia. They trusted him.

But Walsh was becoming increasingly uncomfortable with Kylie and Jason's public displays of affection. So this day he took the pair aside and started up an informal chat about what a special position the two of them were in, and how soon they would be the most popular actors in the country, and about how their lifelong careers in television were already secured. But they had to keep their heads straight, keep their wits about them, play the game. Most importantly, they had to always remember that their prime allegiance was to *Neighbours.*

That said, Walsh dropped his bombshell, a command from above that would fundamentally alter Kylie and Jason's lives for years to come.

Whatever was going on between the two of them off-screen, Walsh told them, if they were intending to continue with their relationship, the public must never find out – it must remain a secret for as long as the two stayed with *Neighbours.* 'If it ever gets out that you're going out together,' warned Walsh, 'it would just ruin the show and the popularity of your characters.'

Kylie and Jason immediately concurred. They had no choice.

Meanwhile, on the other side of reality, Charlene and Scott were having a rough time of those first few months together. Thanks to yet another argument with her mum, Madge, Charlene moved in with Scott's family soon after arriving in Ramsay Street. But Charlene and Scott were constantly fighting, their young relationship suffering many strains.

There was that absurd episode when Charlene turned up one day with a baby, claiming she was the mother. (It turned out the baby belonged to her father's mistress. Madge loved that one, too.) Then there was that fracas where Scott realised Charlene wasn't a virgin, just as he was about to pop her cherry in a hotel room he'd borrowed. How did the schoolboy handle that? Got up, walked out and left Lenie there on the bed, weeping. That earned him a sock on the jaw. (During filming of that scene, Kylie connected a punch that decked Jason. It earned her the nickname of Bruiser on the set.)

By comparison, Kylie and Jason's relationship continued to sail relatively smoothly, despite the network-imposed cone of silence. Even though their public profiles were blossoming, Kylie and Jason still maintained a fairly anonymous existence. While the crowds at their joint public appearances around Australia were growing larger and larger each week, the pair could still walk the city streets of their hometown without the constant interference of fame.

Up until her eighteenth birthday, in 1986, Kylie lived at home with her parents. But now she was hardly spending any time at Mum and Dad's. Most nights after work, it was straight over to Jason's place.

Jason lived in a bungalow at the back of his father's house, on the other side of town. Kylie and Jason would spend an eternity together in this small grungy room over the following couple of years. Kylie loved it, loved lying on the bed listening to records or to Jason practising guitar, loved that he would get up early in the morning to squeeze fresh orange juice and cook bacon and eggs. On some of her increasingly rare days off, Kylie wouldn't emerge from the room at all. As things got crazier and crazier, this messy shack – with its glowing stars stuck on the ceiling – became Kylie's only sanctuary.

Jason had always been a sharp, tough, independent child. Like Kylie, he'd lived out his suburban childhood crowded by someone else's fame. The sole offspring of a former high-profile model and one of Australia's most recognisable television actors, little Jason's birth in 1968 was covered in headlines across the country.

Jason had a fairly happy childhood, but it was no suburban fairytale. Jason's mother, Sue McIntosh (who went on to become a television newsreader), walked out of her boy's life when he was five. For many years, the only contact Jason had with his mum was seeing her for half an hour on TV every night. Until stepmother Marlene arrived on the scene in 1981, Jason had been brought up solely by his father, who was often out of work.

Terence Donovan – the star of such classic Australian cop shows as *Division 4* and *Cop Shop* (he'd later play builder Doug Willis in *Neighbours* between 1990 and 1994) – had always treated his son like an adult. In return, Terry was Jason's confidant, his adviser, the one guy on the planet that Jason truly trusted. Marlene described them as 'an old married couple'.

In his two decades working on television, Terry Donovan had got to know a lot of actresses, but he just couldn't figure Kylie out. He expected Jason to be with someone more mature. After all, it wasn't as if his boy was a novice when it came to women.

On the rare occasions that Kylie ventured out from the bungalow and into the Donovans' communal lounge room, Terry would leap to his feet and perform, cracking jokes and pulling silly faces, jumping over furniture like a monkey – anything to get a reaction out of this shy young woman.

In such instances, Kylie would just stare back at Terry with a bemused, almost embarrassed expression on her face. She would smile politely at his antics, say thank you for everything, and only ever speak when spoken to.

In these earliest months of their relationship, Kylie and Jason virtually spent every minute together. Around the *Neighbours* set, the pair and their secret romance were more entertaining than the drama being created: as soon as the cameras stopped rolling, Kylie and Jason would be off somewhere out of view to hold hands and steal a quiet moment together.

Their hectic daily filming schedules meant that most evenings were spent in the Donovans' bungalow, running through the following day's scenes together. On weekends, if they weren't out of Melbourne on some promotional trip, they'd go to a concert or a club or a film or dinner, just like other teenagers. Mostly there'd be a couple of Jason's old friends in tow; Kylie rarely saw any of her own old friends anymore. On Thursday nights, however, Kylie usually peeled herself off from Jason for a couple of hours to have a sing with a group of other actors from *Neighbours*.

It was fun, lots of fun – the best days of Kylie and Jason's young lives. But as the end of 1986 drew nearer, the honeymoon period lapsed. The two young stars were still in love – after all these months they were still constantly in each other's company – but something had shifted. This perfect love was no longer perfect. Kylie and Jason started arguing regularly.

'Kylie was a really naive, young, pretty innocent sort of girl,' recalled one of the couple's closest friends from the period. 'She had these visions that they were going to get married, that Jason was the one.

'Kylie was always a bit hopeless, not very good at coping on her own. She'd always rely on Jason to help her do things. It was that sort of relationship where someone makes you feel weak. She was very much like that with Jason. Like, "Oh, I'm a hopeless female!" That sort of thing.'

Jason once related to some friends how, on one occasion, Kylie forced him to move his car when he'd stopped in a no-standing zone outside a Sunday market after spending half an hour looking for a park. Kylie insisted it was wrong to do that. Jason told her that he thought the two of them could afford a parking fine but Kylie forced him to move the car nonetheless. 'I'm straight,' Jason confided, 'but she's even straighter.'

Still, for the moment, all these quibbles remained minor tiffs, kids' stuff. Kylie and Jason still loved each other and there was no chance of them breaking up quite yet. After all, who could predict where things would go from here?

51

Certainly not Kylie and Jason. The only thing they knew about their future was that their final stop for 1986 was Bali. The TV station had organised for their new stars to take a couple of weeks off in paradise. Promotions manager Brian Walsh would go along as their chaperone.

At least on an island Kylie and Jason could freely run around for a while holding hands and kissing without fear of public reprisal. 'But remember – be careful,' Brian Walsh constantly reminded the kids. 'No one must ever find out.'

Any remaining doubts about the breadth of Kylie and Jason's sprawling popularity in Australia were washed away one night in mid-April, 1987, exactly a year after Kylie's debut on *Neighbours*.

It was the annual *TV Week* Logies presentation – Australian television's premier awards night, sponsored by the nation's highest-circulating TV guide. Early in the night, Jason was named Best

New Talent on television, nudging out partner Kylie who'd also been nominated in the same category. But the highlight of Kylie's brief career would come within the hour.

By the end of the live-to-air ceremony, Kylie was officially Australian television's most popular actress. At eighteen, she was the youngest recipient of the crown in Logie history. It was the first time Kylie had ever attended a Logie ceremony.

'When it was announced I just went into shock,' Kylie told the press afterwards. 'I certainly don't remember seeing anyone in the room while I was on stage. Honestly, I didn't think I'd win. I just wish I'd been better prepared. I was so nervous and really excited at the time and I forgot to thank all the people in the show. I am really grateful for what I am doing. I am really lucky going from school to a full-time job like this in a show which is so popular. It wasn't until later when somebody asked me what Logie I'd won and I had to actually say it – Most Popular Australian Actress – that I realised how important it was for me.'

Behind the scenes, Kylie's award was at the centre of a hushed-up controversy. Although never revealed to the public, some award insiders claimed that Kylie's co-star on *Neighbours*, Elaine Smith, who played Daphne, had won the ballot for the Most Popular Actress category. But following Smith's run-in with the editor of a magazine in the same publishing stable as *TV Week*, she was snubbed in favour of Kylie. Smith's on-screen partner, Peter O'Brien, who played Shane Ramsay, won the Most Popular Actor award. But these details were of no consequence to Kylie or anyone else. The result was on the board and its effect was immediate.

From its opening days, 1987 gave every indication that it was going to be a golden year for Kylie and Jason. At the start of January, the couple scored their first cover of *TV Week*. That led to others expressing interest in these new teen sensations for the first time. Interview requests started dribbling into the *Neighbours* publicity office.

Suddenly, by Logie night, the media were talking about a Kylie-and-Jason mania. A few days before the awards, the as-yet-uncrowned prince and princess of local television were mobbed by thousands of hysterical young fans while making an appearance at Sydney's Royal Easter Show. Some fifty police were called in to break up the unruly crowd and whisk Kylie and Jason to safety. The two stars were thrown into the back of a police paddy wagon and it took forty minutes to get them out of the venue. Five children were injured in the crush, one girl requiring hospitalisation.

Neighbours fans were becoming more familiar with the real-life people behind Charlene and Scott. Kylie and Jason had already gone public with their opinions on all matter of things. Kylie revealed that she planned to take a fashion design course in the near future, 'in case I need something to fall back on. My grandmother is a good sewer and knitter and she has been teaching me. I learn from my mistakes and the clothes are sort of getting wilder as I go along.'

Jason explained that he was saving every penny to buy a house. Kylie said she'd thought about buying a horse, 'but I knew I wouldn't have time to look after it'. Jason told everyone he wanted to do stage musicals, to follow in his dad's footsteps.

The two kids even got dragged in as spokespeople for a government-funded anti-drugs campaign. 'This is a worthy cause and we're excited to be involved in it,' said a smiling Jason. 'You can relate to it, being young,' added a straight-faced Kylie.

But soon, there was only one thing anyone wanted to know from the pair: 'Are you two going out together?' Every time the question popped up, Kylie and Jason diligently stuck to their script. 'Jason and I are very good friends for sure,' Kylie would say with a smile. 'But as for romance, well, there's too much pressure on us to think about that. It's great to be good friends with someone you work so closely with, though.'

'We're too young to get involved,' Jason would reiterate. 'We want to keep it just as friends, especially as we're working together. I would find it a real hassle playing out our romance on-screen if we also had a relationship off-screen.'

Kylie and Jason were becoming a major craze. A few days after the Logies ceremony, Kylie and Jason made their live singing debuts together at a television anti-drugs concert in Melbourne. Set up by the producers of *Young Talent Time*, the concert saw Kylie and Jason duet on the Howard Jones hit 'No One is to Blame'. Earlier in the concert, Kylie had joined little sister Dannii to sing 'Sisters are Doing It for Themselves'. The two had performed the song together once before, six months earlier, when Kylie made a guest appearance on *Young Talent Time*.

It was around the time of this anti-drug concert that the issue of drugs emerged as Kylie and Jason's greatest private difference. Kylie hated the fact that Jason regularly smoked dope. Outside the odd glass of wine, Kylie hardly ever even drank alcohol. But she never, ever touched dope. She despised it, thought of it as a corrupt substance. And besides, she hated the way it made Jason act like a zombie.

Early on in their relationship, Jason tried to give it up, knowing how much it upset Kylie, but that period of abstinence was short-lived. 'I've always enjoyed a joint, ever since *Neighbours*,' Jason would publicly concede a lot later. 'I'd rather walk into a room of pot smokers than a roomful of alcoholics any day. I think we'd all be a lot better off if marijuana came out of taps across the bar. It just puts a smile on your face at the end of the day, that's all.'

In one of the couple's many rowdy brawls over the matter, Kylie slung Jason's bong out the door. Another time, Jason put his fist through one of the bungalow's walls.

'Kylie feared they'd be exposed as some drug-taking couple,' explained a friend. 'She'd stand there going, "I don't like Jason doing that. What if people find out? We're doing these Say No to Drugs concerts and he's smoking dope."'

There were no such drug-related dramas for Charlene and Scott. Having survived all matter of melodramatic suburban scenes, including an exploding caravan, they battled the conservative natures of their parents and the other leading residents of Ramsay Street over the issue of moving in together. They then prepared to wed.

The marriage of Charlene Mitchell and Scott Robinson was hyped as the wedding of the decade. Their special day finally arrived on Australian television in the first week of July, 1987.   55

Charlene and Scott's wedding show was the highest-rating episode of a soap opera in the history of Australian TV. The morning before it went to air, there was another riot at a public appearance by the couple. Staged in an outer-suburban shopping centre in Sydney, the Charlene and Scott wedding breakfast drew over four thousand frenetic young fans. Again, Kylie and Jason were physically ruffled and had to be escorted from the venue by a cordon of police. Again, fans ended up in hospital.

'I felt really shaken by the danger when the kids went mad and started pushing,' Kylie said afterwards. 'I love the fact that they care about us but we want to be able to do more public appearances without this sort of risk.'

The wedding scene itself was just another day at the office for Kylie and Jason. 'It was a really tiring day,' said the bride. 'I must have walked up and down that aisle twenty times while we were trying to capture the right mood. I'm sure it made a beautiful scene but, for me at the time, I had to think of it as a day's work.

'It was really weird with the wedding,' she added. 'I'd have people come up to me thinking that I was really getting married. They were so excited and their whole lives seemed to be revolving around it. People look up to you so much and I stop and I think, Why? I'm just a normal person and it's a bit frightening in a way that they're all watching everything that you do.'

As for that dynamic 'you-may-now-kiss-the-bride' pash between the new Mr and Mrs Robinson, one *Neighbours* staffer noted that: 'No one's going to believe they're just friends after that.'

Indeed, even the man who had initially insisted on secrecy now felt that things were getting too out of hand – the cover could be blown.

Next thing everyone knew, Kylie had a song on the top of the Australian record charts. Her debut single 'Locomotion', released two weeks after the wedding, in mid-July 1987, would spend nearly two months at number one. The hit record caused everything to become so out of control that the young star found herself in urgent need of a personal manager. Enter Terry Blamey.

Terry Blamey, a 36-year-old booker of cabaret acts, worked out of the Melbourne-based offices of Mushroom Records, the company that had signed Kylie and released her first single.

Blamey had once tasted chart success in Australia with another act he managed, a toothless, square-headed former Australian Rules footballer named Mark 'Jacko' Jackson. Jacko had scored a novelty hit with a song called 'I'm an Individual'. But that was a fluke, and Blamey's main money-spinner was his booking agency, Pace Entertainment.

With 'Locomotion' already at number one, Mushroom executives asked Blamey if he wanted to take on the new singer as a client. Ron Minogue was suspicious of the music industry, and Mushroom figured that Blamey's family-orientated lifestyle would be attractive to the Minogue patriarch.

'Terry was part of the family,' explained Mushroom's managing director at the time, Gary Ashley. 'He was a good, sensible married guy with children, sound with money and a responsible person. He was someone we knew we could work with and someone we felt could work with Ron Minogue. And we had to find a manager for her. Terry was a straight-up guy that we felt would be right. Terry's response in the beginning wasn't "Yeah, yeah, yeah! I'll do it!" He had to be convinced.'

Amanda Pelman, Mushroom's national promotions manager and the person directly responsible for signing Kylie to the label, had handled everything until Blamey's arrival on the scene. Pelman wasn't in a position to manage Kylie herself but never forgot the moment when she gave her star away. 'Blamey came to me,' recalled Pelman, 'and said, "I've heard about this new kid Kylie – has she got a manager?" And I said, "No, no, no – I'm doing it all." And he said, "Oh, do you think I could meet the parents?"'

Years later, Blamey showed his appreciation of Pelman's gracious act by letting one of her bands – teen rockers Indecent Obsession – fill the opening slot on Kylie's European tour. Blamey only charged Pelman a token $US50 000 fee for the honour.

With Pelman's go-ahead, a nod from Ron Minogue and a flat 20 per cent commission guaranteed, Terry Blamey was Kylie's manager.

Many in the cast and crew of *Neighbours* had privately snickered when first told that Kylie was going to release a record. But by the end of August 1987, with 'Locomotion' still on top of the charts, it was Blamey and Mushroom Records who were suddenly calling the shots, running Kylie's life. All of Kylie's spare time evaporated in an endless whirl of media engagements.

Soon, not even *Neighbours* executives could meet with the star without prior consent from Blamey. 'It was the start of many things,' observed a *Neighbours* staffer. 'There were questions of who owned the property. Was Kylie her own identity? Was it Charlene? There were some heated discussions about the use of her time. In the end, Kylie didn't know what her day was – somebody else would tell her what she was doing. You couldn't talk directly with Kylie because she had no idea.'

It was around this period that Kylie started feeling the first strains of fame. Her popularity was now peaking beyond anything she'd ever imagined, but the endless work schedule and pressure were taking their toll. Kylie was getting increasingly stressed, and was constantly falling ill.

'You can lose yourself in all that publicity hype,' the eighteen-year-old actress confessed to a reporter in a reflective moment. 'In the past eighteen months, I have learnt to hide the deepest me. I only show that to very, very close people.

'It's like being a ballet dancer – you have commitments.' (These words of wisdom were obviously borrowed from Kylie's mother, Carol, a former amateur ballerina.) 'Sometimes I think I'd love to work 9 to 5 but then I realise that maybe one day I'll be forced to do that. But I would love to act on stage. I also want to hit the hippie trail and take off up the coast – just sunbake and have a good time.

'When I started on *Neighbours*, I just felt grateful that I had found work. I wanted to be an actress but it had never been one of those burning ambitions that you read about. I was in the right place at the right time. It's that simple. I don't think I'm anything special. I'm like everyone else. I have seen what happens to people who can't and don't cope with the pressure. It's possible to lose what you are.

'There was so much hype around, especially at the time of the wedding. That's when you have to keep yourself separate and not confuse your personality with all the publicity. I realised early on that when it's over, you only have yourself left.'

Jason was always there for Kylie in her times of need, but his girlfriend's recent pop success was making him increasingly twitchy. Jason didn't like the idea of living in Kylie's shadow. He had always wanted to be a rock star – that was his dream.

So immediately there was talk about Jason releasing a single, a cover of an Australian classic called 'The Girl that I Loved'. It never eventuated and Jason would have to wait until early 1988 before he got to sign a record deal – with Kylie's label, Mushroom – and put out a record.

Kylie's recording career, on the other hand, was already booming. In November 1987, with 'Locomotion' having gone to number one in Hong Kong and New Zealand, Kylie took two weeks off *Neighbours* and went to England to record with the world-renowned pop producers Mike Stock, Matt Aitken and Peter Waterman, aka Stock Aitken Waterman, or SAW.

If Kylie's life was insane now, what followed in the first six months of 1988 was pure hell.

By January 1988, *Neighbours* had millions of Britons addicted. At the Australian Bicentennial celebrations in Sydney that month, Kylie got a personal introduction to the Prince and Princess of Wales.

Charles asked his suburban subject what field she was in. Kylie replied that she worked on *Neighbours*. Charles told her he would have to make a point of watching. When it came time to talk to Diana, the most famous person Kylie had ever met, the young entertainer froze up, could only smile and nod, couldn't get out a word. 'I was going to ask her if she watched the show,' Kylie explained later, 'but became a little too nervous and excited. Some people say the royals shouldn't have been here for the celebrations but I disagree. Although I've never been a royal freak, it's an honour to have had them both here.'

By early February, Kylie's second recording, a song entitled 'I Should be so Lucky', was the top-selling single in both Australia and Britain. Kylie was suddenly an international celebrity.

It was all too perfect, too easy. Something had to give. And it only took another couple of weeks for the first genuine disaster of Kylie's career to strike. The fuel for the fire came via a most indirect source. While Kylie and Jason were secretly in Bali at the end of 1986, a tourist snapped the pair together on a beach. Kylie was topless.

Long after the couple had left Bali, the happy holiday pic found its way onto a public photo board at the resort. An Australian traveller recognised the two young TV personalities and swiped the incriminating evidence from the wall. In early March 1988, that photograph, sold by the traveller for $2000, was splashed all over newspapers in Australia and the UK.

Kylie was devastated. There she was standing naked in front of the world. That was the last thing she needed right now. What's more, the picture made an absolute mockery of all the Kylie and Jason 'we're just good friends' bullshit.

The Kylie and Jason camps immediately went into defence mode. 'Kylie can still be my friend without being my lover,' Jason tried to reassure the press. 'We went on holidays together because my mates didn't have any time off, but Kylie had the same schedule as me. No offence to Kylie, but if I was to come home and see her every night and be with her 24 hours a day, I couldn't cope for very long. It's not the way I'd like things to turn out and I think Kylie feels the same. It's hard enough working that closely together on screen.'

Thankfully, things for Kylie and Jason were rushing so quickly now that the incident became just another fragment in an incomprehensible blur of events. At the 1988 Logie awards a couple of weeks later, Kylie scooped the pool, taking out an unprecedented four awards, including the Gold Logie for Most Popular Personality on Australian television, and Most Popular Actress for the second time. Jason was named Most Popular Actor.

All the attention, success, public backlash, scandal, workload, fame – all the facets of life as a celebrity – were quickly causing Kylie to crack up. Kylie was relying heavily on Jason for support but he was busy with his own concerns.

By April, Jason had a manager of his own and went over to London to record with Stock Aitken Waterman. At first, the production team wasn't keen on taking on a male Kylie. Besides, Waterman thought Jason couldn't sing. But under pressure from Mushroom Records, the trio relented and recorded Jason's first record. During that trip, Jason got mobbed by a pack of English schoolgirls while sightseeing at Buckingham Palace. He was becoming an international pop star, the real thing, and loving it.

Through all the hype, there was only one thing Jason insisted the media get straight. 'I've always had an interest in music,' stressed the former member of the Australian Boys Choir. 'Some people have said, "He's following Kylie's success." That's fine for them to say that but if they really looked into my history, they'd understand that it hasn't just started from last year when Kylie released her first single. Even before she talked about recording a song, I had an interest in music.'

Back on the other side, Charlene and Scott had long ago given up their musical ambitions. Now they were just trying to keep their marriage together. The couple's first year as Mr and Mrs Robinson wasn't the best. The dramas just never stopped. Both teens had come close to having extramarital affairs, Charlene with her driving teacher, Scott with his maths tutor. So it was hardly a surprise that when Charlene got news that her grandfather had

61

given her a house in Brisbane, Mrs Robinson shot straight out of Erinsborough and on to the freeway up the coast, making only loose arrangements for Scott, now a cadet reporter, to follow.

In June 1988, with two international hits under her belt, Kylie left *Neighbours*. Her departure coincided with Jason buying a small home in the Melbourne inner-city suburb of Richmond for $180 000. Despite their stresses, Kylie and Jason both knew they couldn't imagine life without each other. So the couple set up house together. But two weeks after filming her last scene for *Neighbours*, Kylie had to leave. She got straight on a plane and took off for a three-month global promotional tour in support of her debut album, *Kylie*.

Refreshed and relaxed at the start of her long voyage, thanks to a couple of weeks away from work, Kylie lapped up her first real taste of the jet-setting lifestyle. Every city received Kylie as a star. But the shine on this new glamour life didn't last long.

Kylie missed Jason. This trip was the first occasion that the two lovers had been separated for any serious length of time since they got together two years earlier. No matter where she was in the world, no matter what was going on around her, Kylie would spend several hours each day talking to Jason on the phone. But it wasn't enough. By August, Kylie was home, stress levels peaking again. The global tour was cut short by a month.

As soon as Kylie touched down in Australia, she set about sorting out her private life. First thing, Kylie now wanted the world to know that she and Jason were an item. She was sick of sneaking around, of all the lying. After all, there was no chance that an official confirmation of their relationship could do any career damage now.

A friend of the couple's recalled one heated argument over the issue during a weekend trip to the snowfields outside Melbourne. 'We were sitting in the car talking about things and then suddenly

Kylie and Jason were at each other's throats [and] she's saying he's always denied he was seeing her.

'And Kylie [then] said, "Look, I think one day we should come out in the open." She goes, "What would happen if we decide to get married? What would we say? Oh, no! We haven't been going out with each other?" Kylie was constantly putting pressure on him about it. She wanted to be known as a couple. It was a topic that was frequently discussed that Kylie used to get pretty shirty about.'

So much so that in September 1988, just a few days after returning from her international promo tour, Kylie – in one of her regular interviews with *TV Week* – took matters into her own hands. Asked about the two being spotted together in an English restaurant, Kylie spilled the beans.

'I guess everyone knows we're going out together,' Kylie finally said aloud for everyone to hear. 'It's just that we've never admitted it before. It's quite true my relationship is very special, but it's for those reasons [that] I don't feel it's anyone else's business. I don't mind people knowing about my career, but I don't see why I should share everything.

'It's good to have a little mystery in your life. Everybody likes a bit of that. It makes you more interesting. We try to avoid anyone seeing us together and try to use different entrances and exists when we're meeting. If everyone knew about Jason and me, then it would spoil the mystique.

'I tell everyone that I'm still living with my mum and dad. That's true because I still take my washing home to Mum and it's nice to have a decent cooked meal every now and then. But I don't live there all the time. I miss being with Jason. That's one of the reasons I don't like going on tour for too long. I really miss him when we're apart.'

It's a pity that Kylie didn't mention anything about this public

63

confession to Jason. Three days after the interview was published, Jason appeared on a live national TV program to talk about the UK success of his debut single, 'Nothing Can Divide Us', which had recently reached number five on the charts over there. When the interviewer inevitably got on to the subject of his relationship with Kylie, Jason blurted out his usual standard denial. When he'd finished, the bemused TV host asked Jason if he'd spotted what Kylie had said in the current edition of *TV Week*. Jason obviously hadn't and sat there speechless, looking like an idiot.

The incident sent Kylie's producers and minders into absolute panic. What the hell was Kylie doing? No one had given the go-ahead to say that sort of stuff. Had she gone absolutely mad? Surely this time, with the grand deception blown out of the water, everything was in dire jeopardy? Like the producers of *Neighbours* before them, Kylie and Jason's music producers were convinced that the kids' constant denial of a relationship was the secret to their success.

Gary Ashley, Mushroom Records' managing director and the man who had introduced Kylie and Jason to SAW, explained the philosophy: 'It was just absolutely the belief, and in turn the belief of the team – and obviously Kylie and Jason went along with it too, they had a brain – that Kylie's whole thing was that everyone wanted to protect her, everybody wanted to love Kylie: she was angelic, she was virginal, every guy could have her, every girl could have her. There was this whole thing about Kylie, that if all of a sudden it was Kylie and Jason, girlfriend and boyfriend, a lot of the myth went.

'And that's why it was maintained. That's just how it was, and whether you believed in it, whether you didn't believe in it, if you were on the Kylie Minogue bandwagon, you went along with it, because it was selling records, it was on the front of papers, it was everywhere. What were you going to do?

'And by the time we started it, we couldn't stop it. If the newspapers had got on to it, she would have been destroyed. Absolutely destroyed. So we'd created our own monster.'

The *TV Week* interview made Kylie's people act desperately. They opted for a hardly innovative damage-control strategy in a last-ditch effort to keep the myth intact. The last line of defence? Pretend the interview never happened, it didn't exist. If there were ever any questions about it, tell them some gutter journalist just made it up. Aside from that, business as usual. Kylie and Jason were not in a relationship. That was official.

This strategy served its purpose. It would be used again many times in the future.

But Kylie didn't care about marketing strategies. She just couldn't believe that Jason had wimped out on their last chance to set the record straight. Kylie felt deeply hurt, betrayed by her soul mate, the one person in her world-gone-crazy who she trusted. This rejection profoundly changed her. Kylie still loved Jason, but it was obvious that he didn't have her best interests at heart.

For the months that followed, Kylie was the saddest she'd ever been. She numbly agreed to go along with whatever everyone wanted for a bit longer. In November 1988, she played out her role in the recording of 'Especially for You', a duet with Jason. The song was a huge hit in many parts of the world over the Christmas period. Kylie also performed her first concert that month, an embarrassing lip-synced affair in a Japanese club in front of three hundred people. Kylie even agreed to rejoin the *Neighbours* cast for one night in London at a Royal Command Performance.

But then, with the arrival of 1989, Kylie started changing, maturing quickly. She didn't cry anymore – there were no tears left to shed. If this was the way of her world, so be it. There was only one thing for Kylie to do – reclaim control of her world.

65

By January 1989, twenty-year-old Kylie Ann Minogue was one of the most successful pop artists in the world. After only a year on the international scene, Kylie had scored big hits in virtually every major record-buying territory around the globe, from the USA to Japan, from Israel to Germany. In the UK, the second-largest record market on earth, Kylie was the highest-selling artist of 1988. Her first five singles had all reached either number one or number two on the UK charts. The album *Kylie* also reached number one.

Kylie and Jason had recently taken a quick holiday together, spending it on the beaches of Byron Bay, a coastal town north of Sydney. Then the two were immediately dispatched to the UK for a whirlwind promotional tour in support of their chart-topping duet, 'Especially for You'. Kylie came home, staying with her family while Jason remained in England and completed work on his debut album, *Ten Good Reasons*.

Meanwhile, in the press, there'd been rumours that Kylie was soon to appear in her first feature film. Her co-star would be David Bowie. This news of a film project wasn't a major surprise. In virtually every interview Kylie had given since becoming an international pop star, she made sure to tell them that now her greatest wish on earth was to make a feature film. In the last days of 1988, Terry Blamey, having turned down all manner of scripts over the previous year, confirmed that Kylie would soon star in her first motion picture. David Bowie, it turned out, was producing and writing the soundtrack.

The next few months flashed by quickly. Immediately after the movie deal was announced, Kylie was off to the US for two weeks of promotion. Then back to Australia. Then Europe. Back home. And so on. From here on, both Kylie and Jason would spend much of 1989 on planes and in cars.

It was in March of that year that Jason finally decided to quit

Neighbours, forcing Scott to leave Erinsborough and head north in a last-ditch effort to save his failing marriage. After all, he'd already left Charlene living alone in Queensland for nearly a year.

Jason had long lost interest in *Neighbours* by the time it came around to filming his last scene. He rolled up on set that final day without having slept – he'd been up all night shooting two new video-clips for the English market. With pre-sales of his debut album topping the 100 000 mark in the UK alone, Jason didn't mind losing the sleep. In fact, as things stood, Jason couldn't have been happier with life.

What's more, Jason loved the new, more sombre Kylie who had emerged over recent months. She hardly ever cried anymore, and she wasn't clingy.

Kylie even looked different. Charlene's trademark puffy curls were long gone. So were Kylie's girl-next-door jeans and T-shirt outfits. Nowadays, in constant consultation with a fashion advisor, even Kylie's most casual wear had taken on a new hint of sophistication. Kylie's face looked different too. The twenty-year-old girl was becoming a beautiful woman.

Kylie and Jason still shared the same bedroom at Jason's house in Melbourne, although Blamey continued to publicly insist that stories of the couple living together were 'pure fiction'. The whole place had been renovated, immaculately set up with all of Kylie and Jason's shared belongings. Scattered throughout its rooms were symbols of Kylie's past life – little covers she'd embroidered for the toilet roll, macramé holders for pot plants, photos of young girls holding flowers. There were no visible signs of Jason's favourite old hobby: his collection of dope plants lived in a tin shed in the backyard.

The nature of Kylie and Jason's relationship had never been the same since that incident where she dared him to publicly declare his love. Kylie grew slightly detached after that, wanting Jason more as a friend than a lover. Together for so long, it was still impossible for Kylie to imagine being forever apart from Jason. There was just so much shared history. Kylie and Jason were the only people on the planet who could comprehend what the other had been through in the last couple of years.

Kylie threw herself into her work with a new focus and a view to taking control of her career. Early in 1989 she'd delivered all her minders the first ultimatum – give me at least my weekends off or this show comes to a close. The guarantee of being able to catch her breath at the end of each week settled Kylie, calmed her, allowed her to jump back on the merry-go-round free of stress.

Once Jason's solo pop career exploded – his debut album *Ten Good Reasons* topping the UK charts and breaking in most of the same markets that Kylie had conquered a year earlier – Kylie and Jason became even further estranged.

When in London together, the two stars still shared an apartment. And when their schedules put them at opposite ends of the globe, Kylie and Jason's minders ensured that the couple spent at least the odd night together once a fortnight. But both Kylie and Jason could have survived without these meetings.

Mushroom's Gary Ashley described Kylie and Jason's relationship at this stage as 'Totally wacko. It was weird. It was like, when did they do it? Did they ever do it? It was too simplistic for anyone.

'They'd get a buzz out of hiring a video and sitting in their room watching it. And you'd think, Okay, they haven't seen each other for a week. And you'd get this phone call saying, "Why don't you come and watch the video with us?" I never felt their relationship was a deeply, sexually passionate affair.'

In mid-April, Kylie started work on her first movie, *The Delinquents*. For the next couple of months, most of her time was spent on location in Queensland. Jason made the odd visit and

Kylie took a few day-trips down to Melbourne. At the end of May, she made the return trip to Melbourne twice in a week – first for her own twenty-first birthday and, the following weekend, for Jason's.

As Kylie would often reiterate in the years to follow, her time spent working on *The Delinquents* was the highlight of her professional career to date. Unlike Kylie's music bosses, the producers of the film constantly referred to their star for suggestions and opinions on the project. The respect they offered Kylie gave her a confidence she'd never felt before.

As soon as filming of *The Delinquents* wrapped up, at the end of June, Kylie was straight off to England to record her second album, *Enjoy Yourself.* Still on a creative high, Kylie tried to have a greater involvement in the creation of her music. But Stock Aitken Waterman would have none of that.

For the following few months, it was back on to the inter-national promotional trail, which eventually landed Kylie in Japan at the start of October, where she was to perform her first major concerts. And that's where INXS singer Michael Hutchence took his cue.

Jason couldn't understand what was going on. Suddenly, Kylie wasn't returning any of his calls. And what was with these weird media mutterings about Kylie being spotted arm-in-arm with the lead singer of INXS? How absurd. What the hell was going on? Jason finally got on to Kylie while she was still in Tokyo, but she wouldn't tell him anything.

A week later, Jason was in America to meet with his record label over there, Atlantic. There'd been a couple more brief conversations with Kylie, who was now in London, but she still wouldn't confirm or deny anything.

Then, the following Saturday night, in a hotel room in New

York, Jason got the call he'd been dreading. It was Kylie. It was all over. She was with Michael now.

Jason was absolutely shattered. His minders tried to cheer their boy up, taking him out and getting him drunk. They even arranged a $10 000 shopping spree in downtown New York. But nothing could snap Jason out of his depression.

For months afterwards, Jason behaved nothing like himself. He was by now a major international pop star, on a par with Kylie in the UK, but suddenly none of that mattered. Jason had never realised how emotionally dependent he'd became on Kylie until the very moment that she dropped him. And that was too late.

Kylie and Jason didn't see or speak to one another again until a couple of weeks after the break-up. The icy reunion came under the stage lights of the *Smash Hits* Readers' Poll Awards in London at the end of October. The two hardly shared a word.

The next time was at the London premiere of *The Delinquents*, in early December. Jason was paranoid that the world media would be watching his every move, waiting for a reaction. So he came to the event prepared.

As Terry Blamey proudly relayed a message to reporters that Kylie was 'disappointed that Michael is not here to join her', Jason made a grand entrance under the arm of a busty Texan model named Denise Lewis.

Kylie and Jason had one more brief meeting, at a SAW recording session in London a few days later when the producers brought together their whole stable of teen stars for a remake of the Live Aid theme, 'Do They Know It's Christmas?'. After that, it would be years before the former lovers' paths crossed again.

Kylie quickly wrote off her years with Jason as kids' stuff. Michael made Kylie feel like a real woman. 'I was tied down to a childhood relationship that went on with Jason and once I got out of that, my world opened up,' Kylie said years later. Indeed, after two exciting, exotic months with Michael, there was about as much chance of Kylie going back to Jason as there was of the actress returning to *Neighbours*.

In the years that followed their break-up, Jason would go on to have a series of short-lived relationships with a stream of beautiful models and actresses. In light of the rapid decay of his recording career, Jason accepted the lead role in a West End production of *Joseph and the Amazing Technicolor Dreamcoat* early in 1992 and pocketed $60 000 a week for eighteen months.

In April 1992, Jason's career was rocked by his successful lawsuit against the British style bible *The Face*. The magazine had printed a photo of him with the caption 'Queer as Fuck'. Jason sued and received close to half a million dollars in damages. When the publication mounted a campaign to stay afloat, it painted Jason 71 as the enemy. The incident caused irreparable damage to Jason's standing among his legions of gay fans as well as in the wider community.

Jason has done little work ever since. Years down the track, having publicly confessed that his relationship with Kylie was a sexual one, Jason tried to be philosophical about that period of his life. 'I used that association to develop my career,' he offered. 'Kylie was just starting to expand that [music] side of her career and I wasn't resentful but it was pulling her away from me, I guess, so I felt a little jealous at various times. But it also gave me an incredible motivation to achieve a similar thing.

'It's been over now for a long time and it will follow us around for the rest of our lives but, God, it was the reason we were successful. We still remain really close friends and that's great.

'We played a game with the media and it worked, it kept them biting. It wasn't meant in a spiteful way, but it was good.'

IT'S APRIL 1987, AND NINETEEN-YEAR-OLD KYLIE, CASUALLY DRESSED IN A MAUVE MOHAIR CARDIGAN AND JEANS, IS SITTING IN THE BOARDROOM OF MUSHROOM RECORDS IN MELBOURNE.

LEARNING YOUR ABC

kylie's 'locomotion'

This is the first time the young actress has set foot inside a record company and she seems somewhat overawed by the gold and platinum disc awards that line the walls around her.

But there's nothing to fear because beside her sits Ron Minogue. An accountant by trade, he's so far acted as a competent de facto manager and financial adviser to both Kylie and her younger sister as they've rapidly and wholesomely risen through the ranks of Australian television fame. Still, this is something new and different for the Minogues – this is the dirty business of rock'n'roll – and Ron seems to have his guard up.

Across from Kylie and Ron sit Gary Ashley, the managing director of Mushroom Records, and Amanda Pelman, the label's national promotions manager.

Kylie looks like she doesn't want to be here. Ashley, for one, definitely doesn't want to be here. This is Pelman's call – she's invited the Minogues to come into the offices for a chat about Kylie's possible future as a Mushroom recording artist. But Pelman has never made a direct signing for the company before and, in her usual forceful manner, has dragged Ashley in for support and to expound the label's philosophy to her guests.

A few days earlier, Pelman had been handed a cassette containing Kylie's demo version of 'The Locomotion', a pop standard co-written by hitmakers Carole King and Gerry Goffin. The song had originally been made a worldwide hit by an American artist named Little Eva back in 1962. Pelman had the tape dumped on her by Mushroom's chairman, Michael Gudinski, who'd simply said: 'I don't know about this. Have a listen. If you want to do it, do it.'

Despite Kylie having recently been voted the most popular actress in Australia, and her face already appearing on magazine covers everywhere, Pelman had never heard of Kylie Minogue when the tape landed in her hands.

She took it home and had a listen. The choice of song, she quickly decided, was brilliant. And it was quite apparent to her that the girl could sing. Impressed enough by what she heard, she turned the television on and, for the first time, watched an episode of Australia's highest-rating program, *Neighbours*.

'I remember thinking, Oh, this is good promotion,' recalled Pelman. 'The concept that someone is on TV and can sing – what a good idea! That was the first thing that made me realise this could really work, because there was this automatic cross-promotion. That's the basis under which I decided to do it.' The next day she phoned Kylie, spoke to Ron and asked them to come and see her.

Pelman had to coerce Gary Ashley to join her in the meeting. Ashley didn't like Kylie's demo at all. But like Pelman, he loved the level of popularity Kylie had garnered with Australian kids. Having agreed to join Pelman at the negotiation table, Ashley was expecting the new talent to be 'a little up-herself bitch and she was totally the opposite. My impression was, "What's not to like? Why wouldn't we do this?" It all looked like it was going to happen easily.'

Long recognised as Australia's premier independent label, Mushroom Records was founded in 1972. Over the years, it had nurtured a reputation for aggressively promoting Australian pop talent as it continually struggled to win its piece of a local music market dominated by the almighty power and influence of subsidiaries of multinational record companies such as CBS (now Sony), WEA (now Warner), RCA (now BMG) and Polygram.

To its credit, and in spite of its tendency for backing cutting-edge acts, Mushroom had its fair share of success. Several of its artists – such as Skyhooks, Split Enz, Paul Kelly, The Models, Hunters and Collectors, and Jimmy Barnes – had been at the forefront of Australian popular culture and provided the label with many hit records on the local charts.

Like many other indie labels around the world, Mushroom had operated in somewhat of an ad hoc manner, its signings directly reflecting the tastes of its head honcho and founder, the brash Michael Gudinski, and those closest to him.

But halfway through the shining corporate eighties, Gudinski started surrendering some of his power to those in the extended Mushroom family that he'd grown to trust implicitly. People like Pelman and Ashley. It changed the face of the label from a purely rock-orientated stable of artists to a company which believed it could now handle artists doing dance records.

Although it was obvious Mr Minogue had little understanding of how a record company worked, he was most concerned with financial matters: how much money would Kylie make? And when would she see the money? How do you pay the money? For her part, Kylie sat there and didn't say a thing.

'So that was a really interesting first meeting,' said Pelman. 'I remember coming out of it thinking, I don't know if this is going to work. I don't know if she really wants to do this.'

But Pelman decided to persist and offered Kylie a recording contract. According to Pelman, some in Mushroom were asking, 'Why would you care?' Others were vehemently against signing an artist of the likes of Kylie, concerned with what it would do to the company's reputation of producing quality music.

However, once the decision was made and contracts signed, Pelman forged ahead, devising a whole image and strategy for her new act. Kylie the singer, Pelman decided, would be marketed directly at young girls.

'It was about finding something that the kids could really get into and the girls could emulate. If a kid in a bedroom could hold her hairbrush high and sing and think, I could do this, then that was fine by me.'

That's what Pelman had done to the music of the Partridge Family and the Monkees when she was a child. Just as Kylie had done to the music of Abba and Olivia Newton-John.

So, strategy in place, the first step was to re-record the demo of 'Locomotion'.

Earlier in the year, Kylie had been given the chance to sing on *Neighbours* when the plot revolved around Scott and Mike forming a band and recording their own demo. Charlene was brought in to do the backing vocals. When the boys played the tape for a record industry head, it was Charlene's voice that received the accolades. But even in the parallel universe of *Neighbours*, the track – a bland composition called 'I Believe', which had been written by Donovan and Guy Pearce – couldn't cut the gravy. Back in the real world, there was talk that the three actors might actually record and release the song, but fortunately nothing eventuated.

Meanwhile, some older cast members – Peter O'Brien, Paul Keane and Alan Dale – had put their own band together, strictly for the purpose of having the occasional play after work. Kylie joined in too, keen to sing.

Then, in August 1986, an old friend of Kylie's, television director and producer Alan Hardy, phoned her up and asked if she would perform at a benefit concert for his beloved Australian Rules football team, Fitzroy. Hardy had played a significant role in Kylie's pre-*Neighbours* career, when he had directed her in *The Sullivans* and cast her in *The Henderson Kids*.

Hardy had already come up with the idea of getting his favourite young actress to do a duet with another local star, the rugged actor John Waters. 'She was really shy about it,' recalled Hardy, 'but they sang "I Got You Babe". And it just knocked everyone out. Everyone was saying this kid's got a great voice.'

The concert was held at a large, barn-like venue, Melbourne's old Festival Hall, and some 1500 supporters of the football team turned out for the event.

'It gave her enormous confidence, this night,' said Hardy. 'She sang one song with a couple of other cast members of *Neighbours* and then they said, "Oh, can we go on and do another?" And they sang "Locomotion" with Kylie out front and, by this stage of the night, she had much more confidence and everyone just loved her.

'Everyone was talking about what a great voice she had, this tiny kid. This big voice coming out of this little girl. She did so well that night, that's where the singing career started. From that they recorded "Locomotion" and away she went.'

Kylie had similar recollections of the night. 'We'd had such a good time on stage that we wanted to do something else. I knew the words to Little Eva's "Locomotion", the backing was simple and the band knew the song, so we raced out and did an impromptu performance.'

In the years to follow, several versions of who was responsible for spotting Kylie's potential on that night and organising to get her into the studio to record 'Locomotion' would be put forward.

According to Terry Blamey, it was Kylie's personal decision to do the demo. A copy of the tape was then given to Mushroom

Records by one of her friends, where it sat in a drawer for two months before anybody did something about it.

Amanda Pelman's memory of events had Kylie going into the studio with co-stars Donovan, Pearce and Craig McLachlan to record the demo of the only song they knew how to play.

Other versions put both Gary Ashley and English producer Mike Duffy (who would eventually record the final version of 'Loco-motion') present at the benefit. Separately, both have been bestowed much kudos as being the talent-spotters who saw Kylie perform that night and got her into the studio.

It was, however, an anonymous, ignored figure in all the 'official' versions of Kylie's story who was responsible for getting her recording career rolling.

This man's name was Greg Petherick.

Greg Petherick, an in-house producer at Channel Ten, had known the Minogue family for nearly a decade by the time Kylie came to work on the show.

For eight years, Petherick was the floor manager on *Young Talent Time*. In the early eighties, he had played a hand in producing an album by another *YTT* musketeer, 'Tiny' Tina Arena. (By the mid-nineties, a bigger Tina Arena was well on her way to becoming an international star in her own right, with minor hits in both the US and UK.)

While still with *YTT*, Petherick had got to know the Minogue family quite well. Ron or Carol would always be around the studio during filming or on the bus when *YTT* went out on tour. On weekends, there'd always be a barbecue or a party that everyone would attend. On a hot night, he might take a dip in the Minogues' pool. Kylie was always around too.

In the middle of 1985, Petherick started thinking about working on another record by a teen artist in the same vein as 'Tiny' Tina.

One day, he shared this thought with *YTT*'s music director, Greg Mills, who suggested that Petherick have a listen to a couple of songs he'd got Dannii's older sister, Kylie, to sing during one of the show's weekly recording sessions. Kylie has said she self-financed these first recordings with her proceeds from *The Henderson Kids*. The songs on the tape included Patti LaBelle's 'New Attitude' and Donna Summer's 'Dim All the Lights'.

Nothing more came of it, but Petherick and the teenager ended up good friends. He drove Kylie to her audition for the part of Charlene. Then, in her first weeks on set, he played the role of Cupid for Kylie, helping the actress snatch the subject of her desire, her handsome leading man, Jason Donovan.

'Kylie came to me and said, "I really like him",' recalled Petherick. 'Then I'd see Jason and say, "What do you think of Kylie?" And he'd say, "Yeah, she's really nice."

'Once it was all on, Kylie brought in a photo that was taken on set of Jason and her. And she wrote on it, "To dear Greg, Thank you very much!" with little lovehearts. And Jason wrote, "Yeah, me too." '

A couple of months earlier, Petherick was responsible for getting together the *Neighbours* band featuring Peter O'Brien, Paul Keane and Alan Dale. Petherick booked a rehearsal studio in inner-city Melbourne and each Thursday night after work, he and the other guys would get together and jam for a few hours, just for the fun of it. When Kylie arrived on the scene, Petherick immediately invited her along.

'We were great mates,' reflected Petherick. 'I said, "Why don't you drop down and have a sing with us?" She said, "Oh, that'd be great." So she came down, sat in the corner and played tambourine for a little while. Then she got up and we did a couple of originals which I'd penned. She sang those and it was good. So she started coming along nearly every week.

kylie's 'locomotion'

'Then Jason wanted to get involved. He used to come down and try to play a bit of guitar, do a bit of singing, which was interesting to say the least. That didn't last long with Jason – he came down a couple of times and that was about it.

'But during one of those rehearsals, Kylie was looking for a song to do. At that time, a lot of bands were starting to do covers and I dragged out Little Eva's "Locomotion", which Kylie had never heard of before, and I said, "Do you want to try that?" So we started doing "Locomotion".'

Soon after her performance at the football club benefit, Kylie stopped attending the weekly jam sessions because 'I kept getting recurring bouts of the flu and was letting the guys down.'

But by this stage, late in 1986, it was obvious to Petherick – and everyone else, for that matter – that Kylie's star was only going to get brighter. This, decided Petherick, was the perfect time to do that record.

'Kylie's character was picking up and I thought, Here's a way to try to make a bit of money, or at least get a record out,' said Petherick. 'And the band wasn't really doing much at that time. So I said to Kylie, "Would you be interested in doing some demos?" '

Through his work in television, Petherick had got to know a lanky blond studio engineer named Kaj Dahlstrom. He phoned Dahlstrom and shared his vision, explaining that 'there's no money in this, but if it goes well, we'll pay you back'.

Dahlstrom, who ran Sing Sing recording studios, had little else on at the time and ageed to enter into the production deal, which made him responsible for recording, producing and picking up the tab for the demo tape.

Dahlstrom set about working out an arrangement for 'Locomotion' – having been told by Petherick that Kylie would sing it in the key of A minor – and brought in a full band of session musicians to record it, including a four-piece brass section.

9

11

12

Piano Bar Disco

What Dahlstrom ended up producing was a funky, big-band backing track, already edited for both a 7-inch single version and 12-inch extended dance version. All Kylie had to do was come in and add her vocals.

When everything was ready, Carol Minogue drove her daughter across town to Sing Sing. Greg Petherick had neatly typed up the lyrics of the song on a piece of paper. But it was all a waste of time. As soon as Kylie heard the backing tape, she knew it had been recorded in the wrong key. 'I can't sing it there,' said Kylie. 'I'll be singing in my boots.'

Kylie and her mum left and Dahlstrom set about bringing all the musicians in again to re-record the track in a higher key – E minor. A week later, everyone was back. This time all was fine and, in about four hours, Kylie had recorded her vocal. 'She came in and we did it line by line because her pitch wasn't exactly 100 per cent in those days,' said Petherick.

'Even though a lot of people knocked her voice in the beginning,' countered Dahlstrom, 'it was obvious she could hold a melody. You could tell her to do something and she would do it. It was obvious she had a lot of potential.' Kylie's vocal from Dahlstrom's recording would later be lifted and used on the version that was released in Australia.

With a copy of the demo tape now in his hands, Petherick set off to see if he could sell his idea and package to a record company. His first call was to Mushroom Records. Mushroom's immediate reply was a resounding 'No way'. 'The comment back was, "No, it's a soapie star, that won't do any good",' said Petherick. 'My idea was, "Well, it's a gimmick record." That's all I wanted to do.'

Deflated by the reaction, Petherick let the whole thing go, not even bothering to shop it around to any other record manufacturers. Then, about a month later, in the last weeks of 1986, he heard from Mushroom again. The label had changed its tune.

'Someone from Mushroom rang and said, "Would you be interested in taking it further?" So I went to see Kylie and she said, "No, not really. I'm not interested at this stage".'

Petherick didn't mind. All his spare time was now being consumed by the *Neighbours* band, which by this stage also regularly featured Craig McLachlan and Guy Pearce. With the sort of public-appearance money now being paid to all *Neighbours* cast members, Petherick figured the *Neighbours* band was a little goldmine waiting to be drilled.

But Kaj Dahlstrom was wondering what the hell was going on. He'd invested $10 000 of his own money into the 'Locomotion' recording and, by the start of 1987, three months after the session, he still hadn't heard a single word back from Petherick regarding the progress of the project.

Dahlstrom called Petherick, who told him the whole thing had died. Anyway, said Petherick, he was no longer interested, he wanted nothing to do with it.

Dahlstrom was pissed off and stuck with a very expensive bit of tape. He sat on it for a bit longer and then phoned Kylie to let her know he was going to shop it around the record companies himself. According to Dahlstrom, 'Kylie said, "Oh, I thought you'd all dropped it. I thought nobody was going to do anything." '

Dahlstrom contacted CBS first up, but they weren't interested in the slightest, merely asking him to put a copy of the tape in the mail. He didn't, figuring that he'd invested so much money into this, it was worth a few minutes of the record company's time. Next he approached a music manager named Glenn Wheatley, who was handling Australia's hottest local recording property at the time, the middle-aged, middle-of-the-road vocalist, John Farnham. One of Wheatley's people told Dahlstrom straight out that the manager wasn't interested in soapie stars.

Still Dahlstrom persisted, meeting with a couple more managers and smaller record companies before getting around to phoning Mushroom's chairman, Michael Gudinski. 'Gudinski told me to come up and play it for him straight off, which I thought was fantastic. So we sat in his office and I played him the tape. But I don't think Michael knew much about dance music at that stage or what they could do for it. He said he'd get back to me in a couple of weeks' time. But then he called me two days later and said, "We should do something." '

It wasn't until a few weeks later, while Dahlstrom was in Perth to watch his brother play a gig, that he heard from Gudinski again. Kylie had been signed and Gudinski was frantic to get his hands on Dahlstrom's multi-track master-tape. Dahlstrom organised for his girlfriend back in Melbourne to take the master into Mushroom, where the English producer Michael Duffy was ready to begin work on re-recording the track.

'Mushroom told me what they wanted,' explained Dahlstrom. 'They wanted a Bananarama-type thing [a Stock Aitken Waterman-produced female dance act] but they wouldn't give me any money to finish it off. Next minute, they gave it to Duffy, and gave him an endless supply of money by the sounds of things.'

Dahlstrom wasn't too fussed, eventually getting his investment back ('Mushroom didn't want to give me anything at first') plus a credit on the record sleeve and a small percentage on the sales of the biggest-selling Australian single of the decade.

'I'm glad Mushroom did it because they did it the right way, bringing in someone from overseas. I don't think it would have hit as big if they'd used my mix. It could have hit big here but I don't think it would have worked in London. If it had gone to somebody other than Mushroom, they might not have done the whole trip, like get Stock, Aitken and Waterman to write songs and do the albums. That was the best thing that could have happened for Kylie.'

One sour note, added Dahlstrom, was that he never heard from Kylie again. 'When it went to number one here, I phoned Kylie up but I couldn't get a hold of her to congratulate her on the whole thing. I think I got her father, because I had their silent number there for a while. But she never returned my calls. She never thanked me or anything and I'd actually shopped the deal for her.'

He did, however, hear again from Greg Petherick, who demanded some reward for his original input. Petherick was furious. The first he'd heard of the project going on without him was when a copy of Kylie's 'Locomotion' arrived in his letterbox.

'Yes, my nose was out of joint with that,' conceded Petherick, 'mainly because no one had come up to me and spoken about it. Not that I had rights on Kylie at all, but you know how it feels – you'd put a bit of time into something and it was your idea.

'I saw Kylie again one time afterwards in the corridor [of the Channel Ten studios]. She had a smile of embarrassment but I didn't want to take it any further. Anyway, I'd dropped off. I didn't pursue the fact that we could have tried other record companies. It was a one-off thing. We'd done the song and I just kept moving on. I never outlaid any money so I didn't really expect anything back.

'People have asked me in the years since, "Was it 'Locomotion?'" But you've got to say it was all *Neighbours*. It wasn't Kylie's ability to sing. She was a great marketable product. Whether it had been "Locomotion" or "Amazing Grace" or whatever else, she would have succeeded. And good for her. I've got great praise for Kylie. She's a great actress more than a singer.

'Kylie and I have never really spoken since. There's no animosity from me but a thank you would have been nice. Even a phone call, a small credit on the record. But there's been nothing. Whether that was a pride thing, guilt, I really don't know.'

Back then, Dahlstrom couldn't offer him any words of encouragement either. Dahlstrom told Petherick he was too late; having pulled out halfway through the project, he was owed absolutely nothing. Anyway, the whole thing was long out of Dahlstrom's hands by then. Mushroom Records was calling all the shots.

As soon as Mushroom Records had the master copy of the 'Locomotion' demo in their possession and producer Mike Duffy available to work on the song, there was a hectic scramble to re-record the track and find a B-side. Mushroom was desperate to have Kylie's debut single ready for release to coincide with the television event of the year – the *Neighbours* wedding of Charlene Mitchell and Scott Robinson.

By now it was June 1987. Mike Duffy had already been in Australia for a short while, working on a variety of local projects that ranged from hard-rock acts to dance-orientated material.

It was the dance stuff that was Duffy's specialty. An employee of Peter Waterman's London-based production house, PWL, Duffy had learnt his trade as a sound engineer over the past couple of years, working on records by European chart-toppers such as Bananarama, Rick Astley, Mel and Kim, and Dead or Alive.

Now Waterman, under an arrangement set up by Mushroom's Gary Ashley, had sent Duffy to Australia to take up a three-month residency at one of Melbourne's leading recording houses, Platinum Studios.

Duffy had never seen or heard of Kylie Minogue when Ashley handed him the 'Locomotion' demo and asked if he thought he could do anything with it. This was Duffy's first solo production gig but he wasn't given much to play with; Ashley and Amanda Pelman had already made it very clear to him what they wanted – one of those synthetic, high-energy dance treatments that had become PWL's stock in trade.

Also quickly dragged into the studio to work on the single was a local musician, Craig Harnath. His band, a rock/dance act called Kids in the Kitchen, was another Mushroom signing handled by Pelman. Duffy had recently also produced some of the Kids' material.

Pelman contacted Harnath the week Kylie's single was to be recorded. She still hadn't found a B-side and was considering a song Harnath had co-written with his bandmate, Claude Carranza. 'So Pelman rang me up,' recalled Harnath, 'with her usual blustering attitude, going: "Glad to be Alive" – I want you to put it on a Kylie Minogue B-side.' It was Tuesday and she wanted it ready by Friday.

'And I'm going, "Well, hang on. Why are you ringing me three days before?" And she goes, "Well, I bloody offered it to V Capri [another Mushroom act]." They wanted to get paid for it. So Pelman, I imagine, would have been like, "Fuck you!" and she would have picked up the phone straightaway and hit my number.'

Over the next few days, Harnath and Carranza put together a backing track for 'Glad to be Alive', a sweet and simple mid-tempo pop song that had taken them a whole half-hour to compose. At the time, both of them were working in Platinum Studios on a new Kids in the Kitchen album, in the room adjacent to where Duffy was now piecing together 'Locomotion'.

Once it was ready, Harnath took a copy of 'Glad to be Alive' over to the Minogue residence to give Kylie her first listen to the track which would make up half of her debut. 'Kylie was still living with her mum at that stage,' said Harnath. 'I'd gone around to the house and had given her the song. She listened to it, had a couple of ideas and changed a couple of things a little bit.'

By the weekend, she was in the studio ready to record her vocal. 'She wasn't there until mid-afternoon,' added Harnath. 'She came in and sang, pretty well carved it in the first vocal. I'm relatively sure it was on the first or second take. Then Claude did backing vocals. There was one bit that was a little too low for her but we didn't really want to change the key because it was going to be a pain in the arse. So we ghosted that with Claude. But it was just a harmony thing, to make it a bit deeper. And, fuck, it was a B-side – who gives a shit anyway?

'I remember I said to her, "So, are you happy with your vocal?" because she was pretty quiet, and she said, "Oh, not really." And I said, "What do you mean? We can do it again if you want." And she goes, "Oh, no – I'm never happy with anything that I do when I sing." And I went, "Okay", because I've had heaps of singers who've said that to me before. And I said to her, "Are you ever happy with your acting?" And she goes, "Oh, no – it's kind of the same thing." I'm sure she's different about it now but it was that whole thing where if you don't assume you're not good enough, you're never going to get any better either.'
87

On the A-side of things, Duffy was having some problems getting 'Locomotion' right. He'd tried simply remixing the demo but it was sounding too human, too many real instruments. By the end of the first day, he'd only succeeded in getting down new bass and percussion tracks, unwittingly using the same session drummer who'd played on the demo. Having already worked with Harnath on co-producing 'Glad to be Alive' and Kids in the Kitchen material, Duffy asked the keyboard player to lend him a hand with 'Locomotion'.

'They couldn't get it to work the way they wanted,' remembered Harnath, 'and Pelman didn't know the terms for what she wanted, but she knew it wasn't right. It wasn't hip enough, because it was a band, real players. So all of a sudden, here I am bloody doing the A-side as well. And I didn't want to do it because I didn't have any deal with them. And it was just worrying me that it was going to be a complete waste of time. It wasn't like anyone was working for free – Mushroom was paying – but it wasn't big money either because, at that stage, Kylie was the first of the soapie thing.

'I suggested that we take all the vocals off the multi and fly them in. It was like, "No, no. No!" But that's what they ended up doing. All they did was pick them up [the vocals from the demo] and drop them back on [the new version] again.

'In the end, I just got so sick of hearing, '*Everybody's doing . . .*' so I just bailed. The thing was that Duffy was pretty head-up on the whole thing because he could see the Stock Aitken and Waterman aspect of it – that's where he was from. It was that thing where any genre starts, most people don't see the potential of it, but who could have predicted the soapie star thing would happen?'

By the time Harnath decided to get out, the song was basically complete. In a single afternoon and evening, Duffy put down the remaining twenty-two tracks of effects to finish it up. Finally, everyone was content. 'Kylie loved it,' said Duffy.

The following weekend, Duffy and Pelman were back in the studio, re-editing the song for the extended, 12-inch dance version. According to Amanda Pelman, the two of them 'literally spent three days, no sleep, doing the 12-inch and really getting into it'. Duffy recalled how 'Amanda was so gung-ho about Kylie.' One of those sleepless nights included rushing off to a nearby nightclub to give the track its first public spin.

'The biggest thing we were always concerned about,' explained Gary Ashley, 'is we had to make the right record. "Locomotion" was either redone or remixed at least four times. And we really worked hard to get it right, to have a hit record. I just remember Michael [Gudinski] coming down and saying, "How much money are you going to spend on this record?" And we were always saying, "No, it's got to be right." '

A week on from the end of recording, it was time for Kylie to make her first music video. Up until this point, Kylie had contributed a total of approximately six hours' work towards her professional recording career.

On Kylie's recommendation, local director Chris Langman was brought in to do the clip for the single. He had directed Kylie in *The Henderson Kids* and they had maintained a friendship in the two years since.

Pelman was happy enough with Kylie's choice. 'I wanted to use someone who was compatible with her,' said Pelman. 'Music-video production in Australia was pretty scatty at the time. Chris was really sympathetic to how Kylie wanted to work. She had her ideas and I had mine. We put them together and Chris was perfect.

'That video,' she continued, 'was set up to make those ten-year-old girls singing into a hairbrush feel comfortable. And feel that they could actually do this too. That's why we made it look like it was a rehearsal.'

89

Filmed in an aeroplane hangar at Essendon airport, on the outskirts of Melbourne, the saccharine-sweet clip put an adrenaline-pumped Kylie in among a cast of six dancers. Wild and wacky, complete with staged 'bloopers', it was merrier than a schoolyard of kids on ecstasy.

The whole Minogue clan was present for the filming. Outside the hangar, two hundred fans gathered to get a glimpse of the starlet. 'I got the impression that she was probably the kind of girl that used to practise being a pop star in front of the mirror,' said Langman, who would go on to direct nearly a dozen clips for Kylie. 'She just seemed to be able to turn it on like that.

'We basically made it up as we went along,' he said of the 'Locomotion' video. 'The only thing I remember about it was that we had to have a bit of product placement in it and Kylie was really against it. It was annoying to me because it meant I had to work out a way of putting it in that didn't look completely obvious. And it was annoying to Kylie as well because she didn't want to know about it. She had it together enough even at that early stage that she didn't want to be used by anybody. She was very paranoid about getting used by people.'

The product placement in the clip – for a body-spray and a clothing retail chain – had been organised by Pelman to cover costs. 'The video was made for no money,' she proudly pointed out. 'I remember going to Gudinski and saying I need ten grand to make this video. And he said, "Forget it! Ten thousand dollars? There's no way." So that's why it happened, to get half the money back. And also I was trying to get Kylie some free clothes out of it. Which I did. She got this big suede coat that she was so happy about.'

It wasn't the only thing Kylie got out of it. 'The art director on that clip,' added Pelman, 'told me the other day that her biggest recollection of making the video was how Kylie went out and bought her own nail-polish to wear in it. She then gave me the receipt and wanted to make sure she got the money back.'

With the recording and video complete, Kylie's debut single, 'Locomotion', was finally released in Australia on 13 July 1987, a fortnight after Scott and Charlene's wedding.

'I can understand that some people are going to be dubious and think, Oh yeah, a soapie star going into music,' Kylie was quoted as saying in the official press release that accompanied review copies of the single to media. 'But it just wouldn't have happended [sic] if it didn't feel right for me. I just felt that it was time that Kylie Minogue stood up to be counted.

'I love what I do in *Neighbours*; it's been a lot of fun and professionally fulfilling. But it's only one thing, one side I want to achieve. In some ways, I feel more at home singing and dancing,

I get to be "me" rather than a scripted character. It really feels like my natural habitat.'

In the wake of Kylie's single, countless other Australian soap stars released records, with varying levels of success. Soap-star pop became a genre in itself. Of course, there was Jason Donovan and other members of the *Neighbours* cast – Craig McLachlan, Guy Pearce, Stefan Dennis (Paul Robinson). A couple of years on, Melissa Tkautz, another soap star, from a short-lived show called *E Street*, had a number one hit in Australia with a dance-pop song called 'Read My Lips'. Melissa openly cited Kylie as her greatest musical influence.

For her part, Kylie never forgot exactly where she was when she heard herself on the radio for the first time. 'I couldn't believe it. It was so exciting. A station in Melbourne used to play the top eight at eight o'clock in the evening. I was at home with my family and I remember I was sitting up on the heater against the wall. And the countdown had already started, so it was probably midway through. Number five, not me. Number four, number three. Come number two, I thought, Oh, I'm not in it. Seriously, God's honour, cross my heart, I thought, Oh, well, I didn't make it into the top eight at eight.

'It did not cross my mind that I would be number one. No, no, no, no. And then the announcement said, "Well, we've got a new entry this week, it's Kylie Minogue . . ." Aaargh! I just squealed. It was just pure relief. I couldn't believe it.'

Within a couple of weeks, the song topped the national Australian singles chart and stayed there for seven weeks. With local sales in excess of 200 000, it became the biggest-selling Australian single of the 1980s.

Kylie would go on to re-record the song one more time, under the direct supervision of Stock Aitken Waterman. The new version of 'Locomotion' (renamed 'The Loco-Motion'), which appeared on

kylie's 'locomotion'

her debut album, was released around the world in mid-1988 as a follow-up to her international debut single, 'I Should be so Lucky'. It had a new B-side, a standard Stock Aitken Waterman production called 'I'll Still be Loving You', which also appeared on the debut album, *Kylie*.

Kylie's 'Loco-Motion' peaked at number two on the UK charts (with sales of 430 000) and number three in the US (with sales topping 500 000). The single also went on to top the charts in Canada, Finland, Ireland, Israel and Japan, as well as going top ten in at least a dozen other countries that had never heard of *Neighbours*.

Indeed, Kylie would ride her 'Locomotion' all the way to international superstardom.

IT'S MARCH 1988, AND THE WORLD SPOT-
LIGHT HAS CAUGHT KYLIE OFF GUARD
AND AT HER MOST FRAGILE. THE SPEED
WITH WHICH HER LIFE HAS CHANGED OVER
THE PAST YEAR HAS LEFT HER DIZZY AND
EXHAUSTED, CONSTANTLY SICK. BEING
FAMOUS IS NOTHING LIKE SHE THOUGHT
IT WOULD BE. RIGHT NOW, IT'S NO FUN
AT ALL.

SO LUCKY

kylie and stress, stock, aitken and waterman

The constant media probing and prodding have caused the first cracks to appear in Kylie's cheery public exterior. She now knows that her dreams of a quiet existence, of settling down, raising a family and setting up a handicrafts store, will have to be put on hold indefinitely.

It's not the acting accolades which are to blame for the Kylie pressure gauge hitting 'Danger'. The whole world knows what's to blame. It's an innocent, infectious little pop ditty ironically entitled 'I Should be so Lucky'.

'I Should be so Lucky', Kylie's second single and her first international release, has been on top of the British charts for six consecutive weeks. It's the first time a solo female artist has had such a stranglehold on the number one spot in Britain since Donna Summer's 1977 hit, 'I Feel Love'. The song also tops the Australian charts, making Kylie the first pop artist ever to simultaneously hold the number one positions in Australia and Britain.

In Australia, 'I Should be so Lucky' has directly followed on from the phenomenal success of 'Locomotion' and shot up the singles chart on the first week of release. But in the UK, where Kylie is still only known as Charlene, 'Lucky' hasn't been an instantaneous hit.

Released in the early weeks of 1988, its debut appearance on the charts was at the bottom of the top 100 and it took a month for the single to peak. Early on the morning of 15 February, Kylie was woken up at her parents' house by a call from PWL, her record company in England, with the news that the song had finally reached its ultimate destination.

Like everyone else, Kylie was initially stunned. 'I have to keep pinching myself to believe it's all happening,' she told reporters that morning. 'I am lucky, lucky to live in a country which affords a young person the opportunity to have a go and make a success of herself.' *Neighbours*, which the BBC had recently moved to a prime late-afternoon timeslot, had become the third-highest rating show in the UK behind the long-running, locally produced soaps, *Coronation Street* and *EastEnders*.

This set the English tabloids scrambling to find some dirt on the new star. In these first few weeks of 1988, they'd already reported that Kylie was anorexic, dropping in weight from 44 kg to 38 kg; she'd had an affair with Australian rock musician Greedy Smith, causing the break-up of his marriage (Kylie had never met him); she hated her mother and her sister Dannii; the vocal on her hit song wasn't her voice at all but the speeded-up tones of another teen idol from PWL, Rick Astley.

Kylie suddenly found herself having to repeatedly deny all these charges. 'They also said I love publicity more than being with my friends,' she said in her own defence. 'As if I would say that.'

All the while, Kylie's workload intensified. Apart from her daily commitment to filming *Neighbours*, she was now constantly fielding interview requests from around the world. Even when she became too ill to work, losing her voice for a week from a throat infection, she wasn't allowed to stop and recuperate. At one stage, her mother had to step in to help out with phone interviews for London, Kylie sitting beside her jotting down answers on a pad.

While elements of the British media criticised their Australian counterparts for what they perceived as soft and sycophantic coverage of the starlet, a homegrown backlash against Kylie was building momentum.

Even though 'I Should be so Lucky' was the most popular song in the country, all but four radio stations in Australia refused to play it, deeming it too twee for their playlists. Several stations began promoting themselves as 'Kylie-free Zones'. Others preferred to give their airtime to parodies such as 'I Could be so Yucky' and 'I'm a Lucky Ducky'. A reader's poll in a local teen pop magazine overwhelmingly voted Kylie as Australia's number one nerd. (The poll also awarded INXS singer Michael Hutchence the title of Australia's yuckiest singer.)

In Melbourne, one backyard entrepreneur started producing 'I Hate Kylie' T-shirts and received thirty orders the first day his classified ad appeared in a local paper. 'I don't think the man putting those T-shirts out hates me,' was Kylie's reaction. 'He's probably making a damn lot of money out of it. It's easy for people who don't know me to say, "I hate Kylie Minogue." But I only value the opinions of people who matter to me, like my friends and family.'

But it was all making Kylie more tense. During a recording session in Melbourne a few days before the Logies, the pressure finally erupted in a flood of tears.

With 'I Should be so Lucky' still on top of the charts and no follow-up in the can, Mike Stock – the Stock in Stock, Aitken and Waterman – had rushed out to Australia to get Kylie to put down vocals for a batch of new songs. Included was 'Got to be Certain', the track which would eventually be released as the next single.

Stock had only briefly met Kylie once before, during the recording of 'Lucky' four months earlier, and was caught off-guard when he arrived in Melbourne to find his stable's latest singing sensation deflated instead of elated.

kylie and stress

'I didn't get through half of what I wanted to do,' said Stock of that trip. 'She was quite tearful at times. She was under a great deal of pressure. I had a girl engineer then, an Aussie girl [Karen Hewitt], and I left them to it one evening, sobbing on each other. They went through a whole box of Kleenex. I let them get on with it. There was nothing I could do. Kylie was nineteen and felt like the whole world was on top of her.'

'I was very tired and emotional when I broke down,' Kylie would later confess. 'I could not carry on. I had the whole world asking, "Who is this girl? We need you to be here." I kept saying, "I'm just a kid from a soapie and I've released a record. What do you want from me?"

'I was forced to grow up fast, get it together and look after myself. I don't think it was a matter of losing control of my life because I didn't have control at the beginning.'

At the time of her breakdown, Kylie complained that she felt like she was thirty. While her parents, her grandparents and Jason tried to keep her spirits up, Kylie couldn't shake off her exhaustion and gloom. The whole situation was compounded by Kylie's smiley face now staring back at her from every magazine and newspaper in Australia.

At the end of March, Kylie flew to London with Terry Blamey and her mother to finish off the work she'd failed to complete during Stock's visit. Any thoughts Kylie had that getting out of Australia would help her escape her problems for a few days evaporated as soon as she stepped off the plane.

During the 24-hour flight from Melbourne, Kylie asked Blamey what he thought awaited them at Heathrow. He told her there was nothing to worry about, to try to get some sleep. Kylie decided she'd put on her sunglasses for the walk through the airport just in case.

Wearing only the shades, an old pair of joggers, a wraparound skirt and her hair tied up in a knot, Kylie found herself exposed to an electrical storm of flashbulbs as soon as she stepped into customs. 'If I had known,' reassessed Blamey afterwards, 'I would have told her a couple of hours before she landed to stop relaxing and prepare herself for a press conference whether you want one or not. I underestimated the Fleet Street press. I learnt from that. It was my fault.'

The following day, London's tabloids were covered in reports of Miss Kylie Minogue's arrival on British soil. The *Daily Express* gossip columnist gleefully described how Kylie had 'looked like a slept-in Qantas blanket'. The writer Jean Rook added that, 'Maybe getting off a plane looking as if you've just crawled out of a kangaroo's pouch is Australian style. The very Down-Under looking Aussie could take lessons from a really high-flying star like Joan Collins, who never lets her image crash by creeping off an 11-hour Hollywood–Heathrow flight like a sleepless wreck. The difficult Aussie teenager has 30 years to catch up to the stature of Joan Collins. On this week's dismal showing, Miss Minogue, long before that, risks becoming a burnt-out old crocodile handbag.' The piece was accompanied by comparative photos of Kylie and Collins arriving at Heathrow.

Later, Kylie admitted to being deeply hurt by that story. 'I got off the plane as myself after a 24-hour flight,' she said. '[Collins] probably had three hours to dress up.' Still, the new star did take a lesson from Collins and would never again walk off a plane in a dishevelled state. (A year later, a more together Kylie would remark to an English journalist that 'I suppose I've always seen myself as a younger version of Joan Collins.')

But there was even more unsavoury media coverage to deal with while in England. The day prior to Kylie's arrival for her 72-hour stay, London's *Sun* had reprinted the infamous topless shot from Bali and filled the column inches with an assessment of the teenager's body shape. On her final day in the UK, another tabloid reported that Kylie had been spat at by a group of girls and almost pushed off a balcony while visiting London's Hippodrome nightclub with her English label owner, Peter Waterman.

All of Kylie's travel stories were flashed back to Australia, giving the local press a whole new angle of questions in preparation for her return. But when Kylie arrived home, just days later, no one was allowed to ask her anything.

Shocked by the reception they had received in London, Terry Blamey placed a media ban on Kylie. All requests for interviews would be rejected. Even the Australian edition of *Time* magazine was refused an audience with Kylie, despite putting her on its cover. 'Presidents of the United States often go out of their way to talk to *Time*,' grumbled the magazine's editor. 'But not Kylie Minogue. She was too tired and too busy.'

Some Australian music industry commentators suggested Blamey was losing his balance on the Kylie treadmill. 'He's one of the few gentlemen in the business,' noted the high-profile Ian 'Molly' Meldrum, 'but it's all got bigger than even he could handle.'

Blamey countered such criticism by vowing that he was quickly adapting to the extraordinary pace and shape of Kylie's success. 'I used to say there was no such thing as too much publicity,' he said. 'I've changed my mind. There is such a thing. I was wrong. People start to get sick of Kylie. They really do. There've been a lot of articles in recent months where journalists have just made things up and it's been damaging. It's been too much. The more exposure you get, the more negative attitudes start to flare out as well.'

Blamey – who compared slagging off Kylie to attacking Shirley Temple – also insisted that his client simply needed a rest. He arranged for Kylie to visit America for the first time, to have a short holiday and meet the staff of the label representing her there, Geffen.

Kylie took a two-week break from *Neighbours* and went off to relax in anonymity in the States. There she shopped and hid. 'She'd just got her new AMEX card and hadn't used it yet,' recalled an American shopping partner. 'At that point, she was worth a lot of money but she'd never splashed out and spent any money on herself. She was sort of looking at these clothes and going, "Oh, I don't know. It's forty bucks for this top. I don't know if I should get it." And we were like, "Get it!" She was like, "Oh, look, I'll put it on American Express." So we took her to these shops and made her buy things.'

Meanwhile, the other side of the Atlantic went Kylie-crazy. 'Lucky' was suddenly a number one hit in countries such as Germany, Israel, Switzerland and Finland. It also reached the top five of another half a dozen European territories.

Then, while Kylie was still in the States, the US market took off. The head of Geffen Records, David Geffen, whose label had a few years earlier drawn John Lennon out of retirement and would later give the world Nirvana, had personally been impressed by what he saw in the video clips for 'Locomotion' and 'Lucky' and decided he'd promote Kylie's records in America.

Once again, even without the assistance of *Neighbours*, the reaction to 'Lucky' was immediate. After the first week of release, it entered the US Billboard charts at number 86 with a bullet and would soon peak at number 28. It looked like, very soon, there would be no place in the world that Kylie could run to hide from her fame.

If Kylie had felt momentarily relieved of some stress during those days in the States, the pressure cooker was turned back on to 'full' when she returned home at the end of April. She was back to working fourteen-hour days on *Neighbours* and psyching herself up to slot in another round of global media interviews in support of the new single, 'Got to be Certain'. It was during these weeks that Kylie and everyone around her accepted that something had to give. Obviously, it would be *Neighbours*.

Soon after her return from America, Kylie talked to the press for the first time since the implementation of the media ban at the start of April. In an exclusive interview with the Melbourne *Sun*, the newspaper which had run some 150 gleaming stories about her over the past year, Kylie – with Jason sitting beside her – confirmed that she would most likely be leaving *Neighbours*. She also tried to be philosophical about the craziness which surrounded her. 'It's better to be talked about than not talked about,' she said in a deadpan voice. 'There were a lot of awful comments in London.

'When you reach a certain height, you have to be pulled down,' she added, having been well briefed by her minders in how to handle the subject. 'I could resign myself to that fact and say, "Well, the time has come where I better go run and hide." But you have to learn not to worry.'

While Kylie said the spitting incident at the Hippodrome had never happened, she admitted there had been instances where she was personally harassed while out in public. 'I was out shopping with a girlfriend and we went into a store. A woman came in and said, "*Neighbours* sucks!" and walked out. I was astounded. I just thought, Who cares what you think? If you don't like the show, don't watch it.'

Within a month, Kylie had turned twenty, filmed her final episode of *Neighbours* and had a second worldwide hit in 'Got to be Certain'. By the end of June she was in London preparing for a two-month promotional world tour. It would still be some time before she'd start to enjoy her life as a world-famous celebrity, but the worst of the trip uphill was now over.

A year later, by which time the constant public and media attention had become the norm, Kylie, in an interview for the Australian edition of *60 Minutes*, candidly reflected on how close she'd come to losing the plot in the early part of 1988.

'There was just so much pressure from so many different people,' she explained. 'I was so sick that I had to have a day off to think about what the hell I was doing. I guess the normal thing would be to say, "Okay, I've had my turn. I'll slide into obscurity." I would have loved to but I couldn't. Because I was contracted, I couldn't stop. I had to keep going.

'I was on everything. I was sick of seeing myself so I thought, The poor public – how are they going to cope? It was overkill and that's when the public turned against me. The public perception was that I was in a soapie, I'm a singer, I'm blonde – I must be dumb. I had everything but I had nothing. It's true what they say about that.'

Further down the track, Kylie would view this transitional phase of her life in a different light. Years later, she described how her head was 'all over the place' during these months and that the whole period had become 'a bit of a blur. But I'm very fond of that time and I'm very thankful. So much success, it's quite amazing. But I do look back and I don't really know that girl too well. Because I feel like I was doing so much, I was so concerned about doing the right thing for everybody else and trying to maintain my sanity at the same time, which I think I did, just. On a couple of occasions I didn't.

'I don't think I had any understanding of how special it was at the time. I realised it was great and I was grateful. But to have a number one single in the UK, for example. Now I know full well how difficult it is to get a number one song in the UK – it's really, really difficult. I guess I was used to being in a number one show and having popularity.

'I realise I worked incredibly hard at that time – I worked myself to the bone. I was anaemic half the time and ill. Working, working, working. But in a way it came very easy, maybe that was because of the hard work. But at the time I didn't fully appreciate it. I was appreciative, but I didn't quite understand.'

Kylie felt like she had everything when she arrived in London for the first time, in October 1987. Back home, she had clinched the boy of her dreams in Jason Donovan, she had a hit record, and she had put a deposit on a half-million dollar house near her parents' home.

Kylie was a star, even more popular than her sister Dannii. She may have been feeling tired, but now she was in England to make a disc with the world-renowned producers SAW. 'Some days I might think, I don't want to do this,' Kylie told a journalist early in the trip. 'But then I reason that I'm one of the luckiest people in Australia and I can't complain. You just don't know what the future holds. That is why I put the pressure aside and just make the most of it.'

Which, for the time being at least, wasn't very difficult: flying first-class to the other side of the world to record a song – this was exactly what Kylie had always fantasised life would be like as a famous singer.

Accompanying Kylie as always was Terry Blamey. The two were met at the airport by Mike Duffy, the SAW house engineer who'd produced 'Locomotion'.

Over the previous year, Mushroom's Gary Ashley had built up a strong working relationship with Peter Waterman, the owner and founder of PWL (Peter Waterman Limited) Productions. He'd met Waterman a couple of years earlier at MIDEM, the annual music convention in France where record companies and music publishers from around the world gather to franchise their copyrights.

Ashley paid Waterman $US7500 for the rights to distribute all PWL records in Australia and New Zealand through Mushroom. By the time Kylie arrived in London, the partnership had already created big hits down under for two of Waterman's acts, Bananarama and Divine.

Since the success of 'Locomotion' in Australia a couple of months earlier, Mushroom Records was lost as to what to do next with Kylie. Back in Melbourne, Amanda Pelman frantically searched for follow-up material. 'I had everybody I could bloody think of writing songs,' said Pelman. 'But it had to be instantaneous. We'd sent a copy of "Locomotion" to Waterman and he rang Gary going, "This is great. I want to do this. Let us write more songs for her." So Stock, Aitken and Waterman sent us over a tape of ten songs and we went, "Right, good idea. Get on a plane." So off she goes.'

According to Ashley, that's not exactly how things panned out. 'I rang Waterman up – I was in the UK on business – and said to him, "I want you to produce a track for me." I said, "We've got this girl, Kylie Minogue, and she's done this version of 'Locomotion'."'

'And he went nuts. Like, "You jerk! You've played with my favourite song. How could you touch 'Locomotion'?" I gave him a copy and he went off: "This is horrendous. This is horrible. I can't believe Mike Duffy had anything to do with this. Blah-blah-blah." It just went on and on. And I was like, "Look, Pete – just do me a song. I just want another hit. I've had a smash hit with her. She's in that show *Neighbours*. So he goes, "All right, all right – send her over. I'll give you a hit."'

Kylie could only afford to spend ten days away from the set of *Neighbours* but Waterman and Ashley had figured that was more than enough time to put down a few new songs. Kylie ended up spending her first few days in London sightseeing and window-shopping, going with Blamey to visit the Tower of

105

London and Madame Tussaud's. Also included was a day-trip to Windsor with her mother's Welsh relatives during which Kylie splashed out on her only souvenir of the trip, a pair of £250 leather boots. She spent the following days locked up in her hotel room, waiting for the call from PWL to tell her it was time to sing.

When over a week had gone by with no word from the studio, Kylie's people started to panic. Something had obviously gone wrong. By the day she was scheduled to fly back home, no work had yet been done. In a panic, Blamey phoned Ashley back in Australia.

'Then, on the last day,' recalled Ashley, 'on the Friday, they were leaving and I rang the studio and Mike Stock answered the phone by sheer fluke. And I told him, "Pete's doing this to me!" And he goes, "Oh my God, I'll have to cancel my sessions. Get her over here."'

So with only hours before they had to be on a plane, Kylie and Blamey caught a taxi to Waterman's Vine Yard studio complex in south London in the vain hope that something could be salvaged from the trip.

The Vine Yard, or the Hit Factory as everyone called it, was headquarters of the PWL musical empire. Waterman had bought the property – located behind the Southwark tube station, a couple of miles from London central – at the start of 1985 for £250 000 and renovated the building to hold four state-of-the-art recording studios, a living area for himself and enough work space for his fifty employees. In the three years since basing himself there, Waterman had become one of the most successful record producers of all time.

Strangely enough, Waterman had very little to do with the music that was being created in his name. That side of the business was left predominantly to his partners, songwriters Mike Stock and

Matt Aitken. They would write, produce and play the instruments on most PWL recordings. Waterman's gift was choosing the right singers to front each song. A former Vine Yard employee summed up the set-up as 'Stock Aitken Waterman with guest vocalists'. Since that day early in 1984 when Stock and Aitken approached Waterman with a demo called 'The Upstroke', the trio had come up with over fifty top 30 hits in the UK.

In the early days, SAW focused on producing cool R&B grooves for the booming English dance market and enjoyed early successes with acts such as Mel and Kim, who topped the UK charts with a song called 'Showing Out', and Princess, who did likewise with the appropriately titled 'Say I'm Your Number One'. Then the label started moving into slightly harder dance sounds through the likes of the bloated drag queen Divine and the eye-patched Dead or Alive. The hits kept coming.

More recently, its speciality had become formularised, electronic bubblegum pop. PWL's roster would soon include such dubious female vocalists as topless model Samantha Fox, the equally well-endowed and musically inept Sinitta, as well as the sixteen-year-old Mandy Smith, child-bride of Rolling Stone bassist Bill Wyman. All released a string of forgettable songs that sounded as if they'd been struck from the same template. Still, these one-hit wonders were attacking the charts as hard as road-tested PWL superstars such as the female trio Bananarama and the baby-faced crooner Rick Astley.

Symbols of the company's continuing prosperity covered the Vine Yard. Countless gold and silver awards hung off every wall, a Formula One car sat near reception, and a real Firestreak missile hung from the building's ceiling. Waterman, a former British rail fireman and the son of a factory worker, now passed his spare time collecting Jaguar cars. He had acquired at least one made in every year since he was born, in 1948.

PWL's approach to music didn't endear it to the pop establishment. Waterman and co. were constantly accused of exploiting their artists, of creating soulless, disposable records that had the passion of a marketing meeting. Critics compared listening to PWL records to eating McDonald's. 'They would no more think of altering their sound than the fast-food chain would allow their staff to play around with the recipe of a Big Mac' was a typical perception.

Waterman didn't care about the critics. Anyway, what they said was basically true and he was proud of it. 'I'm old enough to see the critics having done that to the Beatles and to Motown,' he explained. 'They're my two biggest influences. If twenty years from now, people look back at Stock Aitken Waterman as the Beatles or Motown of the eighties, I'll be very happy. Besides, the critics don't phone the bank manager every week. I do.'

Waterman added that his company's unprecedented success in recent years came from the simple realisation that 'the marketplace was in desperate need of real talent. By that, I mean "ordinary" talent. People just wanted to buy happy-sounding records by people who look good, don't dress scruffily and don't have amazing drug problems.' The company's biggest star, the former PWL tea-boy Rick Astley, was testament to Waterman's theory. Kylie, the next few months would prove, was also 'ordinary' enough to be a SAW star.

But no one could have predicted this as Kylie arrived at the Vine Yard for the first time. Somewhere in the building, Mike Stock and Matt Aitken were busy working on new tracks for Astley and Bananarama when a message came through their studio intercom that a young girl named Kylie Minogue was waiting in reception to record with them. Aitken looked up at Stock as if he'd missed something. 'Who the hell is she?' he asked.

Prior to his conversation with Gary Ashley, Stock had no idea either. He had to put in a call to Waterman, who was in the north of England, to find out what was happening. 'He'd omitted to tell us that she was coming in to record,' recalled Stock. 'He explained she was a girl from a show called *Neighbours*, she was very young, she was a very successful actress, she was very popular, earning bags of money and she wanted to make a record.'

'And she was going back on the plane that day,' added Aitken, 'so we had a bit of a problem. We were very apologetic to her and we said, "Look, there's been a terrible mix-up. Can you give us an hour or two?" And Kylie sat in reception while we knocked up the track that became "I Should be so Lucky". It took us about two hours to get our heads around the problem and then Kylie came in and sang and she was gone in another forty-five minutes.'

Early in those chaotic hours, Aitken suggested to Stock that they simply get Kylie to put down some vocals on one of the backlog of tracks they had lying around the studio. Stock argued that would be wrong, that a new song was needed. Then, according to Aitken, 'I said, "But if we just knock one up, it might not be one of our better ones." And somebody said, "She should be so lucky as to get one of your second-best songs." And from that we got "I Should be so Lucky".'

'We'd actually come up with "Thank Your Lucky Stars",' elaborated Stock, 'and then realised that had already been done. We just liked the idea of "lucky". She was a very lucky girl in what we only knew of her from the surface. It was like with Rick Astley. The only thing we knew about him was that he'd been going out with the same girlfriend since the age of ten. So we made up this song for him, 'Never Gonna Give You Up", which was all about reflecting his relationship with this girl.'

That single had become one of SAW's biggest hits, selling 810 000 copies in the UK alone. 'And that's what we did with Kylie,' said Stock. 'We took something we knew about her and chucked it into the pot. At least we knew that would have some kind of resonance. But these are the things you do when you're desperate.'

In the flurry to complete 'I Should be so Lucky', Stock and Aitken didn't deviate much from their standard pop-song formula. 'Lucky' featured all the songwriting techniques which had by now become their trademarks: a simplistic melodic structure; an uplifting, repetitive chorus; a key-change. The emphasis was very much on that word 'lucky', Kylie uttering it sixty-five times in a little over three minutes. It was pure pop, immediately memorable, as childlike and magical as the Beatles' 'I Want to Hold Your Hand' or the Jackson 5's 'ABC'.

Fatally pressed for time, Kylie had to go into the studio and sing each verse of the song as Aitken wrote the words. While recording her vocals, all Kylie could hear in her headphones was an electronic drumbeat and a bass riff.

Between takes, Kylie was told to wait in the control room. There, visibly nervous and stressed out by what was going on around her, she manicly worked away on her crochet and knitting until called on again to sing another few lines.

By the time she rushed off to Heathrow to make the plane that would get her home in time to start work on *Neighbours* on Monday morning, Kylie still had little idea of what her new single would sound like. As with 'Locomotion', her input into this new recording had been minimal.

With Kylie out of the Vine Yard, Stock and Aitken returned to business as usual, not even bothering to listen to their new song again until the following week when Waterman returned to work. Having mixed the track and added more instruments, Aitken still wasn't sure he liked what the company's new singer had to offer. 'I remember hearing her voice and thinking it was a bit strange. It had a peculiar quality to it.'

Aitken wasn't alone in his reservations about Kylie's vocal talent.

When 'Lucky' was shopped around to the major record labels in the UK in search of a distributor, there was only one taker: London Records made a minimal bid of 12 per cent royalties with no advance. This Kylie girl, PWL was flatly told by everyone else, couldn't sing.

Regardless of what he really thought, Waterman made out that he disagreed. He told everyone he liked Kylie a lot, and thought she had 'an exceptionally good voice and an exceptional ear for music'. Besides, now that *Neighbours* was climbing the British ratings ladder at such a death-defying speed, he knew there was every chance the phenomenal media attention Kylie's peachy-keen image had mustered in Australia might be duplicated in the UK. And that sort of cross-promotion had to be worth a few record sales.

Waterman also claimed he was encouraged by the reaction 'I Should be so Lucky' received when he previewed the song on his weekly show on Capital City Radio in Liverpool. 'I've never seen anything like it,' enthused the hype meister. 'The calls locked the station for about four hours.' But still, without the backing of a big record company, turning 'I Should be so Lucky' into a hit wouldn't be easy.

Essentially a production company, PWL didn't have the infra-structure to distribute records itself. Virtually all of its acts were licensed out to major labels. PWL would provide finished records, right down to the cover artwork, and then one of the majors would take care of everything else, from promoting the artist to getting copies of records into stores. Different PWL acts were handled by different labels. Rick Astley's records, for example, came out through the multinational RCA while Bananarama's carried the London Records sticker.

This state of affairs had already caused Waterman some frustration. Kylie wasn't the first PWL artist to be rejected by virtually the whole record industry. Recently, everyone had also passed on the opportunity to release the debut single by the sixteen-year-old Mrs Wyman, Mandy Smith. Waterman went on to release that record himself, inadvertently taking the first steps in setting up his own label, PWL Records.

But Waterman was adamant that he didn't want to run a record company. When Ashley approached him with the idea that PWL and Mushroom join forces and release 'Lucky' themselves, Waterman blew his stack. 'I'm not starting a fucking record company,' he yelled at Ashley. 'I've lost money on record companies before. This is going to be a production company. All we're going to do is produce artists and license them out.'

Also present in this fiery meeting was David Howells, PWL's managing director and Waterman's main partner in the company. 'I was yelling back at Pete,' recalled Ashley, 'going, "Look, this girl is going to be a star. Why won't you help here?" And David turned around and said, "Gary, go back to your hotel and I'll call you later."

'He called me back at the hotel that night and said, "You send fifteen thousand pounds to our bank account, we'll put up the other fifteen and we'll put the record out ourselves." And they started PWL Records. And I think David Howells put up the money himself. Pete Waterman didn't want to know, and David Howells talked him into it.'

Out of this arrangement also came PAL Productions, a separate company set up by Mushroom and PWL specifically to handle Kylie. At the following MIDEM convention in France, David Howells set up licensing deals for 'Lucky' with labels across Europe.

'It was absurd,' reflected Ashley. 'It was the beginning of a completely absurd situation.'

It's the middle of November 1987, only a couple of weeks after the London recording session of 'I Should be so Lucky'. Kylie is back home in Melbourne, sitting on a four-poster bed. She's wearing exactly the same fluffy white top that she wears in that scene from the film-clip to 'Lucky'.

'Hi!' says Kylie through one of her standard exaggerated smiles. 'Here I am on the set of the video for my film-clip, "I Should be so Lucky". On this video, you'll see what it's really like to make a film-clip. I know it looks like a lot of fun but it's also a lot of hard work. "I Should be so Lucky" I recorded over in London and, believe me, recording the song was just as much fun as making the video.'

Kylie is talking into a camera, recording an introduction for her first commercial long-form video release, a twelve-minute long production that features the clips to 'Locomotion' and 'Lucky' interspersed with Kylie-talk. These are the out-takes.

The voice of Amanda Pelman is heard from off-screen. 'Do it again,' Pelman tells Kylie, 'because you said, "Here's the video for my new film-clip." And it's: "Here's the video for my new *single*." '

The smile drops off Kylie's face. She bows her head and immediately starts practising the sentence repetitively: '*On the set for the video of my new single, on the set . . .*'

The voice of director Chris Langman can be heard in the background, reminding Kylie that the camera is still rolling. Kylie looks away for a moment, takes a breath. As she turns her face back to the lens, the expression she had a second ago transforms itself into another beaming smile. Smiley Kylie is on.

Many who have worked with the woman believe it's this ability to turn herself on and off – what some call Kylie's absolute professionalism – that is the secret to her success.

Gary Ashley observed how it wasn't just a talent she kept for the cameras. 'You could be with Kylie, she could be totally pissed off with the world, she could have had a friend be a complete

113

jerk, she could have been pissed off with me, she could have been pissed with Terry, she could have been crying, you could have been in an elevator with her, she could have been totally pissed off, and the elevator doors would open and you'd walk into a room of thirty press people and she'd be beaming and she'd be incredible. Absolutely incredible. No stony silence at me, best friend, arm in arm, the whole thing.

'Total and utter professionalism. She could turn it on. There were two Kylies. Absolutely. You had to respect her for that mind-blowing ability.'

But for the moment, back on the set, Kylie is struggling to keep it together. 'Hi! I'm on the set . . .' Kylie breaks down laughing. 'Oh, I'm sorry. I'll start again.' She practises the line to herself a couple more times, this time slowly. Then she starts again. And again she cracks up after the first line. 'Oh, shit,' she laughs. 'I'm on this video, film-clip, single. Oh God!'

Pelman suggests they leave it – they got an okay take earlier in the morning. 'I'll just do another one,' insists Kylie, 'because it was pretty awful.' Kylie starts the short monologue again. This time it's near perfect.

Pelman immediately wants to do some cut-aways. She asks Kylie what the day has been like. 'Today has been great,' says Kylie, now looking towards Pelman off-screen. She bursts into laughter again. 'Ask me another question.'

Pelman: 'Um, what's it like working with Chris Langman?'

Kylie: 'Chris Langman is a darling.'

Pelman: 'What's it like making a video? How much involvement did you have in conceptualising the video?'

Kylie: 'There was a fair bit of pre-production which involved people like Amanda Pelman thinking of a concept.'

Kylie warbles on for a few more moments, talking about caterers and lights. Then she mentions that one of the crew gives good massages. She cracks up again. 'Okay, we'll forget that. What was I saying?'

'Start again,' Pelman says sternly. 'What goes into making a video?' Kylie stops laughing. A more serious light enters her eyes. 'What do you want me to say?' she queries without the slightest hint of sarcasm.

'Just do it again,' commands Pelman. 'What goes into making a video?'

The footage is proof that Pelman's hold on Kylie's career was already slackening by this early stage. Throughout the success of 'Locomotion', only months earlier, Pelman was Kylie's guru. After all, Pelman alone could take credit for making Kylie's debut single such a massive Australian hit.

But now, as pressure from all angles closed in on Kylie, she was starting to resent being pushed around by people who didn't take her increasingly sensitive feelings into consideration.

'Amanda had her beliefs and what she felt should be done, and somewhere around this stage, Kylie stopped listening,' confirmed Ashley.

'Terry was involved by now. (Blamey had been Kylie's personal manager for four hectic months.) Amanda had been pushing Kylie, pushing Kylie, do this, do that, and Kylie, even at that young stage, without even really knowing it, she knew what she wanted. And that she didn't want people in her life telling her how to do it. It was pretty early on that Kylie became estranged from Amanda, which was very unfortunate. Amanda is a very forceful person.'

Amanda Pelman's pop-culture genius would be proved once again in the 'I Should be so Lucky' clip. Set in a bright bedroom on a large sound-stage, spruced up with prehistoric computer graphics, it painted Kylie as a thirteen-year-old sample of her target market. That legendary scene with Kylie in a bubble bath was Pelman's idea.

But Pelman would only work on one more project with Kylie, the video for 'Got to be Certain' in March 1988. Pelman devised the clip's storyline one afternoon while sitting in the car outside her house. But by this stage, Pelman was no longer allowed to freely follow her instincts – there were too many chiefs to deal with. In one instance, hours of footage from the 'Certain' clip had to be dumped and re-shot because someone in London didn't like Kylie's hair-do in a scene. On another day of shooting, the talent and crew had to wait on location until a costume arrived in an express package from the UK.

'Everything ended up being generated out of England,' gruffed Pelman. 'Like the first album cover with that fucking hideous hat with no top in it and the hair coming out. That was England. It was going so berserk over there and they couldn't afford to get it wrong. We were just these parochial Australians. What the fuck did we know? It was a bit of that attitude.

'It became a real battle, a real argument about the creative control and who was really going to do this now.'

But the battle was short-lived. From here on in, the image of Kylie belonged to PWL.

KYLIE FACT FILE

circa 1988

Name:	Kylie Ann Minogue
Born:	Star of Bethlehem Hospital, Melbourne, Australia
Birth date:	28 May 1968
Star sign:	Gemini
Height:	152 cm
Nickname:	Bruiser
Colour of eyes:	Blue
Colour of hair:	Natural blonde
Family:	Mum Carol, dad Ron, brother Brendan, sister Danielle
Favourite music:	Prince, soul, funk, R&B
Favourite hobbies:	Relaxing, seeing family and friends
Likes:	Flake chocolate bars, flowers, eyes, cuddly toys, horses, Prince, Thai food
Dislikes:	Heights, brussels sprouts, hanging up clothes, snails, flying, rudeness
Favourite colour:	Mauve

(From a Kylie fanzine, 1989)

CHARLENE MITCHELL IS DEAD.

WOULDN'T CHANGE A THING

kylie versus the world
and its media

Or at least that's what Kylie is thinking. It's early July, 1988, exactly a month since Kylie stabbed everyone's favourite girl-next-door mechanic in the back, dumping her limp image on some beach in Queensland. Now, with Charlene out of the way, Kylie is out to forge a new identity, start afresh. Already, everything has changed.

Kylie is back in London, for the third time in nine months. She's been here for two weeks, ferociously promoting *Kylie*, the title of both her first album and new persona. If we are to take Kylie's word for it, this is the best week of her young life.

Late last month, as Kylie did a final round of Australian media interviews before setting out on this three-month magical mystery tour of the globe, the main concern had been to convince her loyal legion of hometown fans that the big, bad world couldn't change their sweet, happy Kylie. Especially now that Charlene was gone.

'Say I am not deserting them,' Kylie ordered the local press to reassure her impressionable pre-teen followers. 'I am doing this so the album is a success. If they like me, I will keep being me. I am still a normal teenager,' the twenty-year-old insisted. '[But] it's been happening so fast. I can't comprehend it all, which is why it will be good to get away.'

Naturally, Terry Blamey, who would chaperone his prized client on most of her big trip, was also doing his bit to push the new Kylie line. 'Kylie's main concern is her fans,' Blamey shot at one reporter. 'She told me, "I want to do what they'd want me to do." It's not the money – it's what will be the best decision.'

Anyway, right now, if everyone could just keep it together, especially Kylie, they'd all walk away from this caper smiling. Kylie was rested, stronger, over her little nervous breakdown of a few months back. And everybody around the girl now had a taste of how things worked. In the first six months of 1988, they learnt how to exploit the international media, how to work around the traditional music industry. They'd also learned just how hard they could push Kylie before she'd start to crack.

So with *Neighbours* out of the way, with Kylie having accepted her destiny and mastered the rhetoric required for her role as a great pop dictator of the late 1980s, it was time to conquer the world.

An early test of Kylie's new resolve came as she landed at Heathrow Airport, the scene of her greatest publicity defeat only three months earlier. This time around, Kylie appeared fresh and perky as she stepped off the plane from Australia, wearing a mini-skirt and strap-on shoes sprouting big flowers, looking for all money like a young, blonde, clean version of Joan Collins.

Again, a welcoming party of Fleet Street press were there to interrogate the young starlet as soon as she set foot on British soil. 'Why are you here?' they asked. 'Have you killed Charlene?'

The new Kylie kept her well-rehearsed cool, went along with what everyone wanted to hear. No, Charlene is not dead, Kylie told the reporters as she flashed smiles for the cameras. 'It's been left open so if I do decide to go back, the options are there.' Smile. 'I would never be too proud to go back.' Smile.

Of course, the ghost of Charlene would haunt Kylie for several years to come, her unfashionable buffy hair-do and squeaky voice right there on the BBC every day for at least another year and a half. Hell, in Britain, Charlene hadn't even married Scott yet.

Kylie's debut album, *Kylie*, sold 100 000 copies in Britain alone in its first week of release, crashing into the UK charts at number two. It became the fastest-selling album by a female artist in the history of the British recording industry.

Regardless of this achievement, Kylie was still a long way off earning any respect from the English music establishment. At the record-launch party held by PAL Productions in the West End early in July, the guru of English radio, DJ John Peel, chose to interview a life-sized cardboard cut-out of Kylie rather than the real thing, arguing it had far more personality.

Oblivious to these critics, Kylie and her party were obviously ecstatic at the magnitude of the success. 'This is the best week of my life,' declared Kylie. 'I can hardly believe it. The album just doesn't stop selling and looks like being number one.'

For the rest of July, Kylie kept up a rigorous promotional schedule across the UK and Europe, taking in France, Germany, Spain and Denmark. 'The idea of this tour was great,' Smiley Kylie told the press along the way. 'I know it is hard work but what other girl of my age is lucky enough to go around the world?'

But in reality, Kylie was hardly getting to see any daylight, let alone anything of the world. Most days, she was up by seven, straight into an endless stream of press interviews and TV shows, personal appearances and photo ops. It literally didn't stop until she was back in bed by midnight. At that pace, it didn't take long to dawn on Kylie that this actually wasn't much fun at all.

But all the work was continuing to produce startling results. By the end of July 1988, Kylie had claimed the number one spot on the UK album charts, with British sales for her record topping the

330 000 mark. In Australia, *Kylie* peaked at number two, accounting for another 175 000 copies sold. The album also went top ten in several other countries, including Germany, Finland, Denmark, Switzerland, Norway and Israel. Closer to Kylie's home, the record went to number one in New Zealand and number four in Japan and Hong Kong.

Pete Waterman was absolutely loving all this. His company had produced some big stars in recent years but this Kylie thing was on another level. 'Kylie is a phenomenon,' Waterman repeated regularly, happily doing his part to prod the hype monster in the right direction. 'Her records just have the magic touch. She just can't stop selling. Two million copies for every record she makes should not be any problem. The kids just love her. They associate with her so much.'

Meanwhile, the media at home took to labelling Kylie the 'millionairess-next-door'. Estimates suggested that Kylie earned $2.8 million in the first six months of 1988 from record sales alone. Other reports on her financial well-being had Kylie pocketing between $4000 and $20 000 for personal appearances during the promo trip. One story, in the London *Sun*, claimed that Kylie received $23 000 for opening a ride at Alton Towers in Staffordshire, Europe's largest amusement park. 'She is so popular,' grinned Blamey, 'that thousands turn out to see Kylie if she makes a personal appearance at a record store.'

'I knew I would earn a lot more money when I left *Neighbours*,' beamed Kylie when quizzed about the cash. 'I don't want to tell you how much I'm worth, but I am doing great for my age.'

Fact was, Kylie had no idea what she was worth at that point. Neither did her financial man, Ron Minogue. Everyone was talking big bucks but the Minogue family trust had yet to see any of it. But even that minor oversight would be addressed soon enough.

In the last week of July, the SAW version of 'The Loco-Motion' was released around the world. Again, the reaction in the UK was immediate. The single sold close to 200 000 copies in its first week of release there, debuting on the record charts at number two. It was the highest entry ever on the British singles charts by a female vocalist. Of course, 'The Loco-Motion' quickly became a hit everywhere else as well.

So, with Europe conquered, it was time for Kylie to attack America.

It was early August 1988 by the time Kylie landed in the USA. With Blamey taking a break to spend some time with his family in Australia, Kylie was left in the care of the other godfather figure in her life, Gary Ashley.

Back in Australia, there were reports that she had accepted a role in a local television mini-series called *The Silence of Dean Maitland*. Kylie confirmed these rumours, adding that filming was scheduled to commence at the end of the year. 'It's a long way from *Neighbours*,' was Kylie's description of the part in which her character gets seduced by a priest. 'It's a 1950s love story and looks steamier than it is. But I'm not going to do any sex scenes.'

Even sans sex, Kylie didn't hesitate in nominating a couple of actors who would be her ideal priestly leading men. Mel Gibson would be good, suggested Kylie, or how about that Michael Hutchence fellow? After all, Hutchence was receiving rave reviews for his recent acting debut as a junkie, wannabe rock star in the Australian feature film *Dogs in Space*. And it couldn't hurt Kylie's cred in the global music industry to be seen – however innocently – rubbing herself up against one of modern rock's naughty boys. But still, Hutchence as a priest?

By the time Kylie arrived in the States, talk about *The Silence of Dean Maitland* had evaporated, never to be mentioned again.

Kylie was now keen to push the fact that she'd acquired the services of an acting agent in Los Angeles to take over the task of searching out appropriate roles. After all, in regard to her acting career, it was obvious Kylie didn't know what the hell she wanted. 'I would like to do something in America,' she said, 'but I would also like to do a film in Australia. I would like to do something dramatic, a light-hearted movie would be good, and I would like to play someone nasty for a change.'

But Kylie's priority for the time being remained *Kylie*. In the USA, there was still a lot of work to be done if Kylie was to capitalise on the ground broken by the minor success of 'I Should be so Lucky'.

A couple of weeks into the US leg of this gruelling voyage, not having seen Jason or her family in what felt like an eternity, Kylie broke down again and, after a brief stopover in Germany, cancelled the rest of the tour. This time Kylie was just fed up with it all.

'I speak to Mum every day and she sounds really sad,' Kylie told an Australian journalist down the line from the States a few days before pulling the plug.

'There are times when I wish it didn't have to be like this. But now the ball's rolling, I can't stop it. Many a time I would like to send a note from my Mum saying, "Kylie's sick today – she's not coming in", as I could in primary school. But that's impossible. Sometimes I don't know how I retain my sanity.'

'She'd had enough,' analysed Kylie's travel partner, Gary Ashley. 'It wasn't because she was being a cow or anything. She was stuffed.

'It was hell and, by this time, it was wearing pretty thin on Kylie. But we survived. You'd wake up in the morning and England would want phoners [telephone interviews]. You'd work all day on Geffen [Kylie's American label] and then the phone would start from Australia. It was just ridiculous, so absurd. But we survived and she had an absolutely huge hit in America and sold a lot of records. Kylie was fine, she was great, and she worked very hard.'

By November 1988, within a couple of months of Kylie's visit, 'The Loco-Motion' reached number three on the US singles chart. It would be Kylie's last success story in the States. The *Kylie* album, hindered by lacklustre reviews (US music bible, *Billboard*, described the album as 'UK thrush' and said it 'lacked warmth'), only reached number fifty-three. Only one other Kylie record would ever chart in the States – the single 'It's No Secret', which penetrated the top forty in early 1989.

But right now, Kylie wasn't interested in figures. She just wanted to get home.

Kylie was home by late August 1988, cancelling a month's worth 125 of international promotional engagements. The media was again in waiting as Kylie's plane landed in Melbourne, and the girl painted on a brave face.

'I hate to use the old cliché, but I still call Australia home,' Smiley Kylie told the local press corps. Could Kylie explain how it was possible that she was now famous in places that had never seen *Neighbours*? 'I don't know. It's strange.' What makes her so special? 'I think it's a case of being pretty normal that helps.' What was Kylie going to do now? 'I'm just taking it one day at a time.'

A question about her relationship with Jason brought the press conference to an end, a Kylie agent stepping in to explain that she was exhausted after her trip and urgently needed her rest.

But only a couple of days later, a reinvigorated Kylie made her public declaration of love for Jason. Of course, Jason and everyone else forced her to take it back just as quickly.

That embarrassing incident destroyed all Kylie's dreams of a happier future in a flash. While overseas, all Kylie had thought about was getting back to Australia and reclaiming a bit of sanity, a bit of her old life. Now, within days of being home, she realised that was impossible.

Kylie took a break, her first extended leave from work since the start of 1988. But there was no fun to be had. Kylie was growing increasingly detached and paranoid. It didn't help that English journalists now regularly camped themselves outside Kylie and Jason's house for days on end.

Late one night in early October, Kylie travelled over to her parents' house to find that no one was at home. Kylie let herself in. She walked into her old bedroom and was confronted by an intruder rifling through her drawers. Kylie's screams startled the uninvited guest, and sent him crashing through the bedroom windows and out on to the street. Police later hinted the man was most likely a rapist nicknamed the Night Stalker, the man wanted in connection with two dozen attacks on women in the suburbs around the Minogues' home.

By the end of October, Kylie was back overseas again. This trip included her first live appearance in front of an audience since the anti-drugs concert with Jason and Dannii.

Kylie's two gigs were held in a Tokyo nightclub in the first week of November, 1988. On both nights, the singer mimed to recorded versions of six songs from her *Kylie* album. The shows, in which Kylie shared the bill with PWL labelmate Mandy Smith, were hosted by the pop wizard himself, Peter Waterman. The producer remained on stage as each girl danced and pretended to sing. The jolly fat Waterman danced along, trying his hardest to gee up the small crowds. Between sets, Waterman played DJ, pushing all the latest discs from his other singers. During the first night's performance, Kylie had to cut one song short when the tape-machine suddenly stopped, leaving her mid-routine with no music.

A week later, Kylie was back in Australia and went straight into a Sydney studio to record 'Especially for You', her duet with Jason. Neither Kylie or Jason were too keen on the idea of a duet but Peter Waterman was besotted by the idea, claiming he'd already received over 100 000 pre-orders for a record that didn't exist.

'After the wedding went to air in Australia, it levelled out, but in England it's still reaching its peak,' said Jason by way of explaining the couple's about-face in regard to recording a duet. 'So it's the best time to do the song. With the song and the cover of the record, you can tell it's not Scott and Charlene recording a duet - it's Kylie and Jason.'

There was a rush to record the song in time for Christmas, so Peter Waterman and Matt Aitken organised a quick-dash visit to Australia to grab Kylie and Jason's vocals for their guaranteed hit. By the time it was all done, Waterman and Aitken had flown to Australia, recorded the vocals and got back to London within three days.

The trip wasn't all smooth sailing, though. While they were frantically working in the Sydney studio, Ron Minogue cornered Waterman and demanded his daughter's money. How could it be that Kylie was one of the biggest-selling artists in the world and she still hadn't seen one solitary cent?

Waterman and Gary Ashley again tried to explain the situation to Ron Minogue, giving him the reasons why it took years for record royalties to flow through to the artist. But Ron would have nothing of it this time; he was sick of hearing excuses from these music industry con artists. For her part, Kylie couldn't handle the brawling and was in tears, virtually hysterical as she tried to calm her father down. Finally, Waterman had to pull his cheque book out and make a substantial deposit into the Minogue family fund right there on the spot.

In the following couple of days, Kylie and Jason filmed a video for their song. Within a couple of weeks, the pair was back in London, appearing on stage in a Royal Command Performance with the cast of *Neighbours.*

During a stopover in LA on her way back home, Kylie confessed to the *Los Angeles Times* that she wasn't particularly proud of the debut album that had brought her all this wealth and fame. 'I wanted my voice to come through and it doesn't,' said Kylie. 'I feel very removed from this album because I didn't have much say about it and it doesn't sound like me. They did what they thought they had to do to deliver a hit, which they did. But the album still isn't me.'

It was this dissident sentiment that would form the foundation of the 1989-model Kylie.

As the end of 1988 approached, Terry Blamey was driving himself crazy about all the money he'd lost in the last six months. Sure, it had been a good financial year – he had earned more money in the past year than he'd seen all his life. (In 1988, Kylie personally grossed over $5 million, turning over $50 million worth of records, and Blamey owned 20 per cent of that.) But Blamey still despised the fact that there were thousands of bootleggers out there cutting in on his turf.

As Kylie's fame escalated, all sorts of unauthorised merchandising emblazoned with Kylie's image started popping up on shelves across the UK. There were fanzines, magazines, books, posters, T-shirts, even pillow-cases. They were all doing good business, but Kylie and Blamey weren't making a cent from the sale of any of it.

Blamey figured the problem lay in the fact that he and Kylie didn't have control over all those millions of photos taken by Australian newspapers and magazines back in the publicity-hungry years at *Neighbours.* Well, that had to be changed immediately.

11

12

Blamey had a vision – to have every photograph of Kylie under the control of KayDeeBee, the Minogues' family trust. But recently, this vision had led to some farcical scenes. Every time Kylie made a public appearance, Blamey would be sprinting around his client, forcibly shoving his photocopied contracts into the face of anyone pointing a camera her way. It wasn't a very dignified look.

But Blamey was obsessed. He got in touch with photographers who had snapped Kylie in the past and threatened that he would destroy their careers if they dared sell their pictures in Europe. One early target of Blamey's fury was a Melbourne-based photographer named Andrew Lehmann.

The young newspaper snapper had an extensive library of Kylie photos. In the lead-up to the release of 'Locomotion' in Australia in mid-1987, Lehmann was hired by his friend, Amanda Pelman, to shoot all of Kylie's promotional pictures. These sessions included the cover photo of the debut single. Happy with the results, Lehmann was kept on to shoot the cover photo for Kylie's second single, 'I Should be so Lucky'. (Lehmann is the photographer seen in the clip for 'Got to be Certain'.)

But now, less than a year later, Blamey and Mushroom were trying to get Lehmann to hand over all those images of the old Kylie. Lehmann tried to explain that his photos were already in Mushroom's possession – he didn't have anything left. Blamey didn't believe him.

'I got scared, really scared,' confessed Lehmann. 'The bottom line was they came after me and threatened me with all sorts of shit. Legal shit and all sorts of stuff. I got major harassment, all sorts of threats, and basically I ended up signing this form that relinquished all copyright to all the stuff I'd shot of her. It was pretty heavy-duty at the time. And even after I did that, they never employed me again.'

Another photographer from the old days was Greg Noakes. As

a staffer for *TV Week*, Noakes held an expansive, exclusive collection of early Kylie pics.

Terry Blamey and Greg Noakes already shared a fair bit of history long before Kylie came on the scene. The two men had been close friends since meeting a decade earlier. Blamey would often get Noakes to photograph his cabaret bands for Pace Entertainment. As a favour, Noakes had even taken the photos at Blamey's wedding.

Just prior to Kylie's arrival, Noakes photographed the cover of a board game that Blamey had devised in conjunction with an executive from Mushroom Records. The game, which had already been commercially released, was called 'How to be a Rock Star'. The cover depicted Blamey and his partner, Simon Young, along with their wives, dressed up as glam rockers. Blamey was on drums. 'I think that summed Terry up,' quipped Noakes. 'He wanted to be a rock star.'

As recently as the end of 1987, Blamey and Noakes had worked together on putting out the first official Kylie 'biography', a full-colour, 32-page photo magazine aimed at the star's youngest fans. The publication was Noakes' idea and he took all the pictures for it, including shooting the nineteen-year-old Kylie with her family inside the Minogue home.

'Kylie was great,' recalled Noakes. 'We had a good relationship. She really worked hard and we were both very happy with the shots. She was very aware of how she wanted to look. And she did all her own make-up for those photos, she chose the wardrobe.'

The Australia-only magazine immediately sold out. Within a couple of months, once 'I Should be so Lucky' topped the charts in the UK, Blamey organised for a British publisher to release an updated version into the English market. Again, it proved an overwhelming success.

But only a few months after this publishing bonanza, Blamey

was on the line from the London to Noakes in Melbourne, insisting that the photographer hand over his rights to the photos.

Unlike Lehmann, Noakes had openly sold his Kylie pictures to an English photo agency. For a while there, before Kylie's trips to England became the norm, virtually every photo of Kylie that appeared in a British publication belonged to Noakes. But now those same photos were coming up on posters and pillow-cases.

Blamey was furious. 'I never knew how out of hand it got,' offered Noakes in his own defence. 'But Blamey rang up and said, "This has got to stop." I said, "This is the only way I can make money." I certainly didn't get money for doing the work. I got a percentage out of the book.' (Blamey had also subtracted a further percentage of Noakes' profits as an agent's fee.)

'He wanted me to phone up my agency in the UK and say that's enough of that. But he wouldn't tell me why. He wasn't upset with the photos – they were fine. Kylie looked very natural, young, fresh, happy. And in the end he said, "Because we're not making any money out of it." '

Noakes would only ever see Blamey and Kylie one more time. *TV Week* had sent Noakes on a job to shoot the acts appearing on a new TV music show called *Countdown Revolution*. Kylie was one of the acts. 'Terry came into the VIP suite, looked at me and said "G'day." Then he took me around the back to the dressing room to see Kylie. And Kylie was in a foul mood – I'd never seen her in a foul mood before – and she just walked straight through me. And Terry said, "Let's go back and we'll catch up with her later." Then I got word that I wasn't allowed to take photos. And that was it.'

With Noakes flicked out of the loop, Blamey continued to produce official Kylie fanzines for the English market for several years, selling hundreds of thousands of the magazines. The text for the publications was provided by Andrew Watt, a Melbourne-

131

based law graduate and publisher of a weekly music magazine called *InPress*.

Like photographer Andrew Lehmann, Andrew Watt was invited aboard the Kylie project soon after its inception. Amanda Pelman asked Watt to write the press release to accompany the launch of 'Locomotion'. When the idea of the original bio-fanzine came up, Watt was offered its authorship.

'For the first one, I just went to Kylie's house one weeknight,' said Watt. 'She was still filming *Neighbours* at this stage. Her family was all out there having their normal suburban dinner. Once everyone had finished, we went into one of the rooms and did an extended interview based around various topics. It was basically a collaborative interview in that it wasn't just me asking questions and her answering, it was me and her discussing how we were going to say things and what she felt about this, that and the other. She had a lot of input into it. It wasn't just "write what Terry says" sort of thing. Far from it. It really was Kylie doing the talking. So we did that. It took six hours to write.'

Watt ended up writing half a dozen of the bio-fanzines for Blamey, each with increasingly less input from the star herself.

'After the second one, Terry came to me and said it was time to do another one. Kylie was incredibly busy by this stage and I felt that I'd got to know her pretty well. Superficially at least. I felt I knew what she was trying to express and Terry felt confident that I knew what she was trying to express and so, from number three onwards, I basically just wrote them without even sitting down and talking to her. I'd make up quotes for her.

'There was nothing sinister about it. I'd write it, give the text to Terry, he'd read it and go, "Yeah, I'm happy with that." He'd give it to her, she'd read it and occasionally come back and say, "Oh, I wouldn't have quite said it that way – this is how I'd say it." But there was a good trust situation there between me, her and Terry that what I was writing was Kylie-speak.'

During those earliest months of the publicity chaos, Watt also inadvertently became Kylie's undercover press agent. At the request of Pelman, Watt acted as the Minogue camp's double agent in among the press corps. Whenever Kylie called a press conference in Melbourne, Andrew Watt would be there in the crowd with his tape recorder and specific assignment brief.

'It was Amanda's idea, I guess,' offered Watt, 'but we sort of had an unwritten system whereby if there was some real smart-alec journalist that was trying to give Kylie a hard time, she'd know that I was there as some sort of safety valve. If someone was really going on about Jason and topless photos or something, she'd know to look over and I'd come up with something simple like a "So, what's it like to work with Stock Aitken Waterman?" type question. I did that a couple of times at Amanda's request and at my own discretion.

'But with time, I noticed Kylie was getting more and more comfortable with handling that sort of stuff. And I remember vividly that one day there was a press conference at a hotel and some prickly topic came up and I thought, Oh, here we go, stick up the hand and get ready to ask an easy question. And she looked over and smiled and just signalled not to worry about it. And at that point I thought, Great, she doesn't need even that subtle form of media protection anymore. She can handle herself and she knows it.'

In the years to follow, Kylie would evolve into the consummate media performer. Blamey, on the other hand, never quite achieved his vision of controlling every Kylie photo in the world. But he got pretty close.

By the end of 1989, Blamey had set up an infrastructure whereby every publication doing a major story on Kylie was provided with its own exclusive, prepackaged photo shoot of the star. This way,

133

Kylie Inc. always retained copyright of the photos, could practise some quality control, eliminate boot-legging and keep everybody happy.

(In years to come, Blamey would push the envelope further. By the mid-nineties era of the shamelessly tabloid Dannii, he'd streamlined things to such a degree that magazines purchasing inside information from one of Dannii's loose-lipped 'friends' would also be supplied with photos, at a price. Editors of such magazines believed Blamey always got his cut of the talk money, too.)

Coincidentally, it was late in 1989, during Kylie's promotion for *The Delinquents*, that Kylie faced her last great media embarrassment. Asked in an interview what she thought about the political situation in South Africa, Kylie replied: 'I wish they'd stop killing the rhinos.'

The absurd comment would be thrown back in her face for years to come. Kylie took the standard denial stance on the matter: it wasn't what she'd said at all. 'It's complete bullshit,' she said. 'I was talking about animals. For God's sake, if I was talking about South Africa, I probably wouldn't have been talking about the rhinos. It was just fucked. Completely fucked, because that's playing with someone's intelligence, which really pisses me off. Obviously the journalist, whoever it is, has a deep hatred for me.'

Despite Kylie's protests, the reporter involved, a writer for Australia's *Dolly* magazine, has always maintained that's exactly what Kylie said. So she misinterpreted the question. What was the big deal? There was no malice intended.

It probably helped explain what Blamey meant when he said that Kylie was too honest in interviews for her own good.

IT'S A SATURDAY NIGHT IN LATE MAY 1989,

AND A STERN-FACED KYLIE ANN MINOGUE,

DRESSED IN A SHORT, CHIC, GLITTERING

BLACK EVENING DRESS EMBROIDERED

WITH PLATINUM FLOWERS, ARRIVES AT

HER TWENTY-FIRST BIRTHDAY PARTY IN

MELBOURNE IN A WHITE MERCEDES BENZ.

THE DELINQUENTS

kylie's coming of age

Jason Donovan, who earlier in the week knocked Kylie off the top of the British charts, has flown back to Melbourne from London especially. The prince of pop is somewhere in the back seat, but in the ensuing media jostle, no one seems to notice. This is Kylie's night.

Kylie has been a nervous wreck all week, freaking out that this evening would turn out a disaster. 'It's all exciting but also it's pretty scary, all this attention,' Kylie quipped in the lead-up to the event. 'Because I think, What am I going to do after I'm twenty-one – I'm going to have to act like I'm an adult and have no excuses to act like a kid.'

Inside the Red Eagle Hotel, a trendy bar on Melbourne's beachfront, Kylie's history lies in wait for her. Outside, a pack of thirty paparazzi are making it a struggle to get near the door. Kylie had so much wanted this to be a private, intimate affair, but that was never going to happen.

Inside, one hundred and sixty of Kylie's friends and business acquaintances are gathered to wish their famous girl a happy birthday. A new, adult Kylie seizes the night and turns it into a final farewell to her suburban past.

Throughout the party, Kylie methodically works her way around the room, taking the time to have a chat with literally everyone in the building. When it comes time to make a speech, Kylie successfully holds back her tears, explaining to the congregation that she's sorry she can't spend more time with them. It's an emotional goodbye.

'I didn't feel it was a great night,' murmured one party-goer. 'It wasn't on a grand scale. I remember thinking, Wow, for someone who has got all this money, they could have had a better party.'

'It wasn't a grand bash,' agreed another guest. 'Jason's twenty-first [held a week later in a nearby renovated church] was a groovier and hipper sort of thing. The pair of them were pretty conservative with their money, had pretty tight pockets.'

Kylie ended up leaving her $100 000 party by 2.30 a.m. She had to be up early in the morning to fly to Queensland and take up her new life. Just like Charlene had done. Up there in Queensland, the adult Kylie was already halfway through filming her motion-picture debut, *The Delinquents*. Again, everything about Kylie's life was changing rapidly, but this time, for the first time, Kylie was at the controls of the change.

It was in late April 1989, almost exactly a month before Kylie's twenty-first birthday, that the international production of *The Delinquents* was officially announced to the world.

After an initial two weeks of pre-production, a press conference was held in Sydney where the film's two stars, Kylie and American actor Charlie Schlatter, were introduced to an assembled throng of international media. There was only one thing anyone really wanted to know. Will we see Kylie naked? 'That's what they're asking me to do,' Kylie answered casually. 'But nothing too explicit. We're aiming for an M [Mature audience only] rating. So I won't be stripped.'

After the press conference, Kylie confided to one journalist, her old unofficial press agent Andrew Watt, that she was finding the whole move into film acting 'a bit nerve-racking because there are a lot of expectations on me. Even if I do a good job it'll be hung on me anyway so that's not going to worry me.

'So I'm trying not to think of what will happen after I've done it. I'm trying to concentrate on doing the best that I can do. The question they kept going on about today was "How are the fans going to react to me changing from sweet, innocent squeaky-clean Kylie to this girl that has sex and has an abortion and smokes?" I was trying to get it through to them that it's not me. I'm acting and it's just me keeping moving as an actress.'

Kylie's co-star, Charlie Schlatter, was a late starter on the *Delinquents* project. No sooner had he read the script and accepted the part than he was on a plane heading for the other side of the world to start filming. He'd never heard of Kylie Minogue before he landed in Australia, but very quickly realised exactly whose party he was crashing.

Schlatter's own profile back in America had recently received a boost when he played Michael J. Fox's little brother in the Hollywood production of *Bright Lights, Big City*. Previously, Schlatter had worked with George Burns, playing the decrepit comic's teenage incarnation in *18 Again*.

But from the moment he met the media in Australia, Schlatter understood that no one was interested in anything some two-bit Yank actor had to tell them unless it was details about Kylie.

Within a week of the press conference, on the first day of May, Kylie and Schlatter moved into the small Queensland country town of Maryborough, which had been transformed to act as the set of *The Delinquents*. The sleepy sugar-cane town immediately fell victim to an annoying plague it had never experienced before – international paparazzi.

The first day of filming ended with a party to celebrate Schlatter's twenty-third birthday. Kylie would afterwards describe her co-star as 'just the life of the set. He was very loud and very American and always playing around'.

By the end of the first week, the quick-witted young American had acquired a patter to deal with the constant Kylie quizzing. 'I've only known Kylie for a week but every day we get closer and closer,' grinned Schlatter. 'She's been riding on the handlebars of my bike a lot. Actually, we have to do it in the movie so we're practising. But we took off for a while once and Kylie's management were a little worried. I think it would be safe to say I'm developing a healthy crush on Kylie. Part of me would definitely like her to be my girlfriend.'

For Kylie, the initial anxiety about launching her film career spilled over into those first few days on location. She later admitted that, 'I was completely insecure for the first week because I knew the crew and other actors would have preconceived ideas about this prima donna bitch Kylie Minogue and what I would be like.'

To the contrary, Kylie made quite a first impression on her fellow cast and crew, helped by her insistence on picking up the bill for Schlatter's impromptu birthday party on that first night. 'Kylie was very generous, very much the leading lady, which was very impressive,' recalled *Delinquents* co-star Todd Boyce.

'Kylie's workload was enormous but she was totally on top of it. She was picking up her moves before anybody. She was completely focused and right there. She was going to bed early and getting up early. She didn't have a lot of time for going out at night and she was concentrating on the job.'

In Boyce's mind, *The Delinquents*' two leading actors made for a strange match. 'Kylie and Charlie were from entirely different backgrounds in terms of their egos,' he explained. 'Charlie was the Evian-water-bottle-toting, rat-pack product and Kylie had a very strong Australian-worker, practical sensibility. She was very much the professional. Although she possessed a lot of star quality, she didn't seem to need or want to be treated that way, which was delightful.

'They were opposite ends of the coins that way. Charlie was more predisposed to being treated like a star and expected it more than Kylie, who seemed to be secure in her own right.'

On this new job, Kylie was constantly being asked for her opinion on every aspect of the project's production and to consider every single gesture she was making to the camera, to explore the art of acting. Here, it didn't matter if it took a whole day to get a scene exactly right.

Kylie's keenness and her natural ability to soak up information and instructions impressed everyone. *Delinquents*' director Chris Thomson noted how Kylie 'focuses intensely on whatever she's trying to find, and she usually nails it very well. She's a considerable actress, capable of a much greater emotional range than anyone you normally see in the soapies. She was sitting next to me at the press conference and I felt this rush of adrenaline just take her over. She does the same thing for the camera.'

Meanwhile, the rest of the *Delinquents* cast and crew were happy to treat Kylie with the respect they felt befitted a performer of her stature and even temperament. And it didn't hurt Kylie's standing on the set when, during the first week of filming, news came through that her sixth international single, 'Hand on Your Heart', had made it to the top spot on the British charts. It was Kylie's third British number one in sixteen months. Her other three singles all reached number two.

Kylie had a ball in that first month of filming. In comparison to the frenetic pace of the last few years, Kylie considered all this to be quite leisurely. Mum Carol was always around and Jason made a visit, too, but he couldn't stay long – he was a very busy boy these days.

Kylie arrived back on the set after her twenty-first birthday do in Melbourne, and the cast and crew threw the star another party. Kylie loved it, had a better time than the night before. There was still another three weeks of filming but this past month had been without question the happiest few weeks of Kylie's life so far. She'd learned so much, was finally starting to feel free of all the constant anxiety and pressure in her life.

This was what Kylie wanted her world to be like forever. It was exactly the sort of joyful, fairytale lifestyle that Kylie had always dreamed of but long stopped believing in. Having now seen that such a world was attainable, Kylie set about making sure that no one could ever take such happiness away from her again.

'I don't know what to think of my performance,' Kylie confided to a journalist as the shoot in Queensland started wrapping up. 'I don't have that much confidence in myself. People say, "Aw, come on. You must have confidence." But not really. I bluff my way through most of it. I guess I'm most worried because if the film gets panned, I'll be in the firing line. Not the producers or anyone else – it'll be me who gets slammed.'

Kylie joined the cast of *The Delinquents* in December 1988. Formal contracts were signed in a meeting at Warner Brothers Studios in Los Angeles. But the story of how *The Delinquents* ended up being a Hollywood production started long before that day.

The Delinquents was based on a debut novel by an Australian author named Deirdre Cash, who wrote under the pen-name of Criena Rohan. Published in 1962, a year before the writer's death, *The Delinquents* told the unfortunate story of Lola Lovell, the character Kylie would play in the film version.

Set in outback Queensland in the mid-1950s, the tale tells the story of Lola's life from the ages of thirteen to twenty-one. It traces the path of a child rebelling against the overbearing authority figures that rule her world. The one thing that keeps the girl alive is her forbidden love for the seafaring youth, Brownie Hansen (Schlatter's character). The two eventually end up living happily ever after.

A couple of fledgling Australian film producers, Mike Wilcox and Alex Cutler, acquired the movie rights to *The Delinquents* in the mid-1980s. The two envisioned their film version as a grimy, arty, rock'n'roll *Romeo and Juliet* on celluloid. For years, the pair's efforts to raise money to get the project into production had come to no avail. Then in October of 1987 came an unexpected break.

Music superstar David Bowie, who'd recently appeared in big-budget films such as *Absolute Beginners* and *Labyrinth*, was asked during a press conference if he had any intentions of taking on more movie work. Bowie explained that he'd recently read a book called *The Delinquents* and he was keen to find out who held its film rights.

143

Wilcox and Cutler immediately got in touch and Bowie offered his moral support in getting the project off the ground. Armed with that, the producers spent another year securing the necessary money. By the end of 1988, a major Australian film distributor, Village Roadshow, a subsidiary of the American entertainment giant Warner, committed itself to bank-roll the movie on the condition that Kylie Minogue got the lead role.

Wilcox and Cutler had already considered approaching Kylie with the part of Lola Lovell – they'd also considered Nicole Kidman – but Village Roadshow was insistent that it had to be the singer. Independently of the two producers, the company secured Kylie's services before throwing its financial weight behind the film.

During Kylie's time on *Neighbours*, Terry Blamey received hundreds of unsolicited filmscripts from around the world. Blamey didn't bother passing most of them on to his client.

But the script of *The Delinquents* appealed to Blamey from the moment it was handed to him by an old acquaintance who worked at Village Roadshow. It looked like it was the perfect vehicle to launch Kylie as a film star. The association with Bowie wasn't likely to hurt the young pop singer's other career either.

Kylie backed up her manager's view about all the other scripts. 'I had heaps of trashy movie offers before this came along,' she said. 'They just wanted my name to get bums on seats. But this story is beautiful and very touching. I certainly see it as a serious story.'

The people from Village Roadshow viewed Kylie's association with the project somewhat differently. 'We decided to make this not just a small Australian picture, but a picture with international value and impact, and the way to do this was to cast it up,' boasted one executive as it was revealed that the mother company, Warner America, intended to make *The Delinquents* one of its priority international releases.

Warner immediately insisted that a few minor adjustments be made to the production notes. First and foremost, an American boy had to be cast in the role of Brownie. This posed something of a problem, as the Australian producers had already offered the part to another actor who'd duly accepted it. Ben Mendelsohn, the Australian actor who co-starred with Kylie way back on *The Henderson Kids* and *Fame and Misfortune*, had to be paid a kill-fee to make way for Charlie Schlatter to enter the picture only a couple of weeks before filming was scheduled to begin.

At the time, co-producer Mike Wilcox defended the late change against charges of corporate sell-out slung at him by Australian critics. 'There have been instances of Australian films using imported elements where it has been totally grating and totally inappropriate,' offered Wilcox. 'But I believe you can employ an American actor and make it work.'

Wilcox would later change his opinion on the matter. With the benefit of hindsight, the producer mused that he believed 'Charlie Schlatter's engagement, in a sense, hurt the credibility of the film. In retrospect, I would have much preferred Ben Mendelsohn do it. That was my preference at the time as well. It's just that when your distributor is also a major investor, you are susceptible to their attitudes on what the key casting ought to be.

'It might have got a better public reception if it had been a 100 per cent Australian project. The public is very sensitive to that and doesn't always react well to foreign elements in those roles, especially in what was essentially a very Australian story.'

In the end, the final version of *The Delinquents* bore little resemblance to what its Australian producers had initially conceived. Even David Bowie withdrew his association with the project before production was complete. During shooting in Queensland, executives from Warner America faxed the set on a daily basis, constantly demanding that the script be purged of its most blatant Australianisms. For example, the word 'dunny' had to be replaced by 'bathroom' and so on.

Despite a commendable and emotional performance from Kylie, *The Delinquents* suffered immensely from this perpetual watering-down of the original story. The completed version of the $8 million production was wooden, riddled with clichés, and failed to generate much energy.

Kylie was seemingly oblivious to all this. During the two months of filming, she only had a couple of concerns. One was the reaction she'd get from her character having an abortion. 'Parents of fans have come up to me during filming and asked about the abortion scene,' she said. 'They don't want their children to see it. I tell them it's not shown in detail. Thank God!'

Kylie was quick to point out it could have been a lot worse. In the book, Lola had two abortions. 'If we'd left it the way it was, it was so depressing that you'd have wanted to slash your wrists

kylie's coming of age

after seeing the film. We've tried to liven it up, so there's only one pregnancy termination – things like that have made a lot of difference.'

Kylie's other primary concern was the question of nudity. While Schlatter was happy to hype the film as 'Very sexy – it will make most people remember what they felt like the first time they made love and lost their virginity', Kylie played that aspect down as much as she could.

'It's not about getting your clothes off,' she said. 'It's about young people learning about their sexuality. It's very tasteful. And I don't think this film will shock young people because it's about them and rebelling.

'There are several love scenes. Lola is very passionate. The film is the story of their love, but if people are expecting all revealing shots, there's just not. You just catch a glimpse of virtually nothing. It's all really tasteful. I wouldn't have let it through if it wasn't.'

When *The Delinquents* was eventually released to the public in December 1989, reviewers seemed to disagree with Kylie's assessment of things. The film critic from London's *Daily Mail*, Corrina Honan, was particularly scathing. 'Images stick in the gullet,' wrote Honan. 'The fifteen-year-old Kylie character Lola (cliché *Lolita* connotations here) being driven to the abortion clinic by her evil and selfish mother; Lola staggering out after the abortion, barely able to walk; sheet-tossing sex scenes five minutes (or so it seems) after boy meets girl; bare breasts and buttocks; sex, sex and more sex, with Kylie's crackling and cockatoo whooping.'

Honan added that *The Delinquents* may come across as 'Tame to an adult film-goer but even the most liberal-minded parents have a duty to think deeply before exposing impressionable children to this tosh. Armed with Kylie and its British 12 certificate, it is, I think, immoral and dangerous.'

'Ultimately, *The Delinquents* is a weakly handled, insubstantial film,' stated another critic. 'Kylie has as much acting charisma as cold porridge,' offered London's *Daily Mirror*. 'Pulp fiction manipulated by an army of fat cats counting shekels behind the myth that is Minogue,' added *Today*. None of this stopped *The Delinquents* topping box-office receipts in Britain over Christmas 1989. It ranked third in Australia, and completely flopped in the USA.

All the way through filming, Kylie had steeled herself in anticipation of this sort of cold critical response to her film. She knew the harsh criticism was inevitable, regardless of either the depth of her performance or the quality of the product itself. Ultimately, none of the slagging bothered Kylie. By the time *The Delinquents* hit the cinemas, Kylie had met Michael Hutchence.

Suddenly, Kylie was conveying a totally different attitude about the film, and everything else about her life for that matter. 'I am proud of the film, I really am,' she insisted in the week leading up to *The Delinquents*' world premiere in London on 5 December. 'I think it's fantastic and I have to stick to that. If people hate it and it's a flop, well, that's all there is to it. But I worked hard and really looked inside myself for new emotions. The film will always be a very special memory for me.

'There are a few parts in the movie that are going to shock people,' boasted the newly confident Kylie. 'Which is good. I like to do what people don't expect.' This was the same girl who only a year earlier emphasised that, 'I would like to try a lot of different things but there is no point moving faster than your audience.'

There was one other niggling issue that Kylie felt she had to put to rest once and for all. 'My character is nothing like Charlene from *Neighbours*. I know that will shock some people but that's exactly what I wanted to get away from.

'I've had a lot of offers where the characters were like Charlene but I wanted a change. I can't go on being scared to step out. I thought this film was the right move to make. Charlene was sweet but I want to expand as an actress and take on roles with more depth. If it means tackling raunchy love scenes, then why not? That's what you do when you're an actress.'

Filming of *The Delinquents* in Queensland concluded on 23 June 1989. By the end of the following year, it had been released on home video.

Producer Mike Wilcox never found out if his project ended up making a profit. 'There's a lot of mythology around about *The Delinquents* which I find pretty disturbing,' said Wilcox. 'One of them is this idea of it being a box-office failure. I wonder where these people get their information from because I was part of the production and I don't have accurate figures on what its performance was. I think the jury is still out on whether it was a financial failure or not.'

Within a fortnight of the conclusion of filming, *The Delinquents* was out of Kylie's mind altogether. Kylie suddenly found herself back under the thumbs of Stock Aitken Waterman at the Vine Yard studios in London, recording her second album, *Enjoy Yourself.*

Kylie headed for England early in July 1989, armed with the conviction to claim a greater say in her musical career. While still filming *The Delinquents*, Kylie had felt increasingly embarrassed each time she was forced to confess that she had no idea what her next record was going to sound like.

'I've been told it's a bit more soulful and funky,' was all Kylie could offer. 'I'll find out the details when I get there. That's how we work.'

Regardless, Kylie remained vocally loyal to her arrangement with Stock Aitken Waterman. 'People love to think I've been manipulated, that I'm thoughtless, manufactured, overproduced. At the start, I didn't know much about SAW or how the music industry operated. Now I've got more knowledge and people expect me to leave them.

'I haven't written my own songs yet but my answer to the people who criticise me for not doing that is, hey, when I'm ready. Stock, Aitken and Waterman are good at doing that and I must be good at bringing it across in a way people can relate to and enjoy.

'We cop a lot of flak because we're commercial but you have to have a lot of talent to be commercial. I'm sure there are a lot of arty-farty people who would love to be commercial and sell millions of records rather than twenty. Maybe they don't have what it takes, maybe I don't have what it takes to be arty-farty but that doesn't worry me.'

By the time the Kylie entourage pulled up in London for recording, it had gained a new regular in Sydney-based stylist Nicole Bonython. Kylie had first met Bonython a couple of years earlier during the singer's first-ever photo shoot, for the Australian edition of *Rolling Stone*. Bonython's husband, Grant Matthews, took the pictures. The husband-and-wife team photographed Kylie on several other occasions and the star eventually asked Bonython to come on board as a permanent personal fashion consultant.

Kylie was immediately proud of the results of this new set-up. 'In the last few months, people have noticed my change in style – that's fantastic,' beamed Kylie. 'It was a specific move, done on purpose. I could have done that sooner but it was worthwhile waiting so I could have more impact. The change could have been too understated or too over the top.

'I'm really comfortable with the image I project now. Style is your own interpretation of what you are and what you want to project to others. Often what you are isn't what you project.'

'Kylie calls the shots, no matter what she's doing,' explained Nicole Bonython. 'I might select fifty items of clothing and Kylie

149

might choose fifteen from that. The kind of pop star she is, everything has to keep changing. She uses me so she can keep up to the minute.

'Kylie's changed a lot over the last year or so. Her knowledge of things now, and not just with clothes and shoes, is incredible. She's gotten a lot tougher in her dealings with people. She used to get intimidated. But she doesn't anymore. She's the one that pushes people around. But in a really nice way.

'Kylie is really diplomatic, totally dignified, even when you know she thinks some of the people around her are totally fucked. She's professional, and her image is that she has to be really nice all the time. She maintains that, no matter how tired she is.'

Decked out with her new look and new attitude, Kylie strolled into the Vine Yard studios to begin work on *Enjoy Yourself*. Instantly, she realised it was going to take more than a new dress and hairstyle to sway SAW from its old ways.

It was instantly obvious to everyone at the Vine Yard that Kylie had done a lot of growing up since she was in making the first album, just over a year earlier. SAW didn't like their artists making changes without authorisation. Gary Ashley explained that SAW wanted Kylie to remain 'a robot that did everything they told her to do. Because they had a vision, they had a plan, they had an approach. In the real world, they also wanted a robot that looked great, could speak great, could perform great and could think great in terms of giving intelligent responses in interviews. The two don't marry.

'By this stage, Kylie didn't want to be messed over by anybody anymore. She wanted to control the image she was projecting. And she wanted to approve her artwork and she wanted to hear what songs she was going to record and she wanted to hear her mixes. It was a very natural progression for any artist to make.'

Kylie's new music was still being created in the same ad hoc manner that defined her first recording session with SAW. Phil Harding, one of Kylie's regular studio engineers at the Vine Yard, described how the production line worked: 'Mike [Stock], Matt [Aitken] and Pete [Waterman] were capable of getting things done very quickly. They'd knock up a track and get Kylie in to sing a verse and a chorus and decide whether it was happening and then get her to sit outside and wait while they wrote the rest of it.

'It was pretty harrowing for some of the artists, the way they were treated as if they were on a production line like that. All Kylie would sing to, for instance, was a very rough drum beat, a keyboard and a rough bass. Get her to do her vocals and then, once she's done, send her off and get backing vocalists in and more keyboard players and try and finish off the record around that. And then the guys mixing the records would mix them overnight. In two or three days you'd have a record.'

And SAW weren't interested in letting some little girl with an image crisis interrupt that highly successful, slick process. This was a source of much tension.

'There was one occasion where we'd half-written something and Kylie was hanging around,' recalled Aitken. 'There was a bit of pressure in the time department and I kindly asked Kylie if she wouldn't mind leaving us alone. I think she took offence at that.'

'I can remember that instance,' added Stock. 'Kylie got very upset by that. You have to develop a relationship with your co-writers and basically we were under pressure to finish this song. So Matt said, "Go on, Kylie – fuck off!" It sounded harder than it was meant.'

Whatever the case, the incident marked the beginning of the end of Kylie's association with SAW. By the end of July 1989, about three weeks after Kylie arrived at the Vine Yard, *Enjoy Yourself* was complete. The end of the session coincided with the release of Kylie's seventh single, 'Wouldn't Change a Thing'. The new single debuted at number two on the UK charts.

Enjoy Yourself was released in the UK early in October 1989 to coincide with a series of live shows Kylie had scheduled to perform across England and Japan. With guaranteed pre-sales of 600 000 copies, *Enjoy Yourself* debuted on the top spot of the British charts. By Christmas, it had sold double that amount.

By the end of October, *Enjoy Yourself* had reached number ten on the Australian charts, number five in Japan, one in Hong Kong, two in Greece, three in Belgium, four in Norway and ten in Denmark.

Publicly, Kylie remained reserved on her opinion about the new album. 'With *Enjoy Yourself,* I said to them, "I want to be able to sing on it",' she told Australian *Rolling Stone.* 'And yeah, I am clouded by computers a lot of the time, but that's pop music. And I don't want to just drop pop music. I like it. *Enjoy Yourself* is a step in the right direction and with the next one I want to take a leap, because I've got new confidence in myself and I think I'll have something more to offer.'

Between finishing the record in July and going into rehearsals for her fourteen-date 'Roadshow' tour in late September, Kylie was back out on the road working an intense international promotional schedule. 'Yesterday I had breakfast in Sweden, lunch in Denmark and dinner in England,' she grinned along the way. 'If you had told me that when I was a child, I wouldn't have believed you.'

Kylie had finally acquired the mind-set necessary to deal with this sort of existence. She was also starting to overflow with this new-found confidence, and loved being surrounded by aides who were hand-picked. Aside from the 'artistic differences' with her music producers, Kylie was thoroughly enjoying this more relaxed version of fame in which she was calling some of the shots.

Kylie was already making plans for the new decade. SAW were

talking about writing a musical for her, but Kylie had decided she wanted to quickly make another movie, a comedy. 'It would be just great,' she enthused. 'I don't think I'm funny at all. I'm pretty witty – I don't know about funny – but I'd like to do a comedy.'

But all these plans came to nothing. The unexpected events surrounding Kylie's 'Roadshow' tour in Japan at the start of October ensured that no aspect of Kylie's life would ever be completely predictable again.

KYLIE ANN MINOGUE IS REBORN.

BETTER THE DEVIL YOU KNOW

kylie and michael and sex and drugs and rock'n'roll

It's a few days short of the end of the 1980s and 21-year-old Kylie, sporting a short-cropped platinum wig and a tiny black cocktail dress emblazoned with a metallic noughts-and-crosses game, arrives at the Australian premiere of *The Delinquents* in Sydney in the back of a big, beat-up old American Dodge. You can almost feel the foundations of popular culture rattle as Kylie emerges from the car arm-in-arm with INXS lead singer Michael Hutchence.

It's a surreal scene. Kylie is virtually unrecognisable as the girl who only a year ago was swooning 'Especially for You' beside beau Jason. Now looking sultry and sophisticated, Kylie is dwarfed by the scruffy Michael, her head glued to his chest as the pair briefly pose for photographers outside the cinema. The media is in a frenzy. Kylie and Michael together – six months earlier, this would have been completely inconceivable, an absurd prediction.

In the time it takes the invited guests to sit through the film and move on to the post-premiere party, the story and first official images of superstardom's latest odd couple have already been flashed across Australian TV news bulletins.

Hi world, meet the new Kylie.

Everything about Kylie's life changed from the moment she hooked up with Michael Kelland Hutchence.

Born in Sydney on 20 January 1960, Michael was eight years older than Kylie. The eldest son of a salesman and an ex-model, Michael had a nomadic childhood. When he was four, he moved with his family to Hong Kong, not returning to Sydney again until he was twelve. When he was fifteen, his parents split and Michael moved with his mother to Los Angeles for a year. Soon after his return home again, Michael and some friends formed a band that, by 1979, was called INXS.

In the years leading up to INXS, Michael had been besotted by punk culture. As far back as anyone could remember, the charismatic, intelligent young lad had trampled and trashed his way through life behaving like a rock star, long before the little punk had any right to do so.

Mocked as a Jim Morrison wannabe early on, Michael, with time and practice, developed his own unique take on rock's traditional image and mastered the art of projecting it. He became the sort of rock'n'roll frontman that, with a single gesture, could make a stadium full of girls swoon and get the boys punching the air. 'I am a fucking great rock star,' Michael once shamelessly declared to a journalist. Indeed he was.

Kylie met Michael for the first time in July 1987. It all happened so quickly, so unexpectedly. The incident left Kylie speechless, absolutely starstruck. The setting was the post-awards party of the last annual Countdown Music Awards ceremony in Sydney.

By that point, INXS had already staked a serious claim to being Australia's biggest rock act of the decade. A long-time favourite of local kids, the band's 1985 album, *Listen Like Thieves*, sold over a million copies in the USA. That same year, INXS headlined Australia's musical contribution to the global Live Aid concert. The band's next album, 1987's *Kick*, went on to sell seven million copies worldwide.

Michael was sharing a loud joke and a drink with a group of

friends at the awards when Kylie quietly slipped into the room. Neither initially noticed the other. Kylie was invited along courtesy of the fact that 'Locomotion' was currently sitting at number one on the Australian charts.

On arriving, Kylie started star-gazing, running her eyes around the room in an effort to spot some of her favourites. Suddenly, a hysterical, screaming man leapt in front of her.

It took Kylie a moment to realise that this guy was yelling directly at her but she couldn't catch what he was saying. It took Kylie another moment to focus and realise that this guy was Michael Hutchence. Kylie was startled, caught completely off-guard. Michael said something else, this time more quietly and with a smile. In the next instant, he disappeared back into the crowd. Kylie was spellbound.

'I thoroughly enjoyed the Countdown awards,' Kylie enthused   157 soon afterwards. 'I was worried that a lot of the famous big-time rock music people would look down on me as just a soapie star moving in on their area and zooming up the chart. But they were all really nice. Michael Hutchence made an effort to come over and say hi, which was good of him.'

'It was absolutely hilarious,' recalled one of Michael's entourage. 'The moment Michael saw her, he jumped up and started running at her with his arms waving and shouting, "I want to fuck you! I want to fuck you!" It was just hilarious.'

Kylie met Michael again about a year later, towards the end of 1988. INXS had just returned to Australia after a long and fruitful international tour, which included picking up five MTV awards in America, and was currently in the middle of a sell-out run of stadium shows around the country.

Kylie and Jason went to see the band perform in Melbourne. Jason was a big INXS fan. A friend of Michael's saw the young couple at the concert and invited them back to the after-show party at the band's inner-city hotel.

'There were these gangster guys there from Chicago, there was a lot of drugs,' recalled the middle-man. 'I think Michael changed Jason and Kylie's lives dramatically in one night. Jason was like, "Oh, this is great. Lots of pot." And Michael was just getting Jason shit-faced so he could sit on the bed and talk to Kylie all night.' (Michael later explained: 'I was apologising to her. I've given her heaps in the press.')

'Michael set himself a new goal on that night,' said the rock star's friend. 'Then he just went and chased her in Japan.'

Kylie's third and most significant encounter with Michael came a year later, this time in Hong Kong.

It was the end of September 1989 when Kylie arrived in town with Carol Minogue and Terry Blamey. In a few days, on 2 October, Kylie was scheduled to perform the first concert of her first international tour. The fourteen-date 'Disco in Dreams' roadshow would start in Nagoya, play four shows in Japan, and then move on to the UK.

Kylie had spent the last few weeks of September rehearsing for the tour with her four back-up dancers in London. There was no band – Kylie would sing live to back-up tapes. She went early to Hong Kong to make a guest appearance at the Miss Asia-Pacific beauty contest and take a short break before the start of the tour.

Michael, who was living in Hong Kong at the time, heard that Kylie was in town and sought her out. When he finally found her, Michael acted like the perfect gentleman, leading Kylie and her chaperones on a guided tour of the city and taking them out on his boat for some water-skiing.

Kylie had never had so much fun. But before she left, Michael made sure that she was clear on one thing: he had chosen Kylie to be his next lover.

A week later, on 6 October, the night the Kylie roadshow played to 40 000 people in a baseball stadium in Tokyo, Michael appeared again, this time in Kylie's hotel room.

'Kylie had a big suite at this hotel, and all of a sudden, in walks Michael,' recalled Gary Ashley. 'I'm like, he was in Hong Kong last week, he's in Japan today. Sure! Then it was like, "Let's go clubbing!" So whoever was around, I think there would have been about twelve of us, walked from the hotel to this club.

'And Terry Blamey and I were walking at the back, and Kylie and Michael were walking up the steet ahead of us. And Michael was trying to hold her hand. And she kept slapping it away. By the end of the night, they were arm in arm. That's when it began.'

159

Kylie and Michael spent the next few days together. They avoided Jason's phone calls and became lovers. But Kylie had to dash off quickly. Her first English show, at London's Hammersmith Palais, was scheduled for 15 October. Kylie and Michael made plans to meet each other again in Hong Kong once the tour was over. By the time the pair returned to Australia in early November 1989, Kylie was a different human being.

'Michael Hutchence turned that girl on her head,' observed Ashley. 'It was the wildest transformation you would ever want to see in your life. Weeks. We're talking about an immediate, instant change.

'Kylie started dressing differently, started looking different, started doing her hair differently. She sexually awoke. She became another person. Attitudes changed, everything changed. She changed her circle of friends – she was hanging out with an entirely different set of people – and you could see that this was completely changing her direction.

'Michael musically woke her up, sexually woke her up, image-wise woke her up – circle of friends, the whole thing. I don't even know if Michael's aware of just how much of an impact he had on her. But it was all there waiting to happen. He didn't put it in her. It was there already.'

'It's probably the last thing we should have done,' offered a gleeful Michael soon after his relationship with Kylie became public knowledge. 'But it just happened. We come from totally different situations. And obviously all this affects me because I don't have that sort of image. People are saying, "What the hell are you two doing together?" I guess it shows how cruel I am, because I don't really care.'

Kylie and Michael spent a week alone in Hong Kong following the end of Kylie's British tour and then landed together in Sydney at the start of November 1989. Michael had come back home with INXS to record the band's follow-up to *Kick*, eventually entitled *X*. Kylie had no intention of letting him out of her sight.

In the short time they'd spent together so far, Michael had already succeeded in completely reprogramming Kylie's take on the world. Kylie fascinated Michael. He'd never met anyone like her. Kylie's extraordinary tales from her recent, tortured past entranced him. To every new anecdote, Michael would shriek: 'Fuck off! You're a star! Stop letting them treat you like that!'

'She's a really strong person,' Michael would gush. 'She's formed her own philosophies because of all that. It's made her a really good person because she can cut through people so fast that it's not funny. It's scary how much she's toughening up.'

Michael's view of things immediately made an impression on Kylie. To her, everything about his interpretation on how to play the fame game sounded so much more appealing and exotic. Kylie wanted to play on Michael's side.

As always, Kylie adapted quickly to her new environment. Friends of Michael noticed how Kylie had immediately adopted some of his mannerisms, like brushing her fringe out of her eyes with the back of her hand.

Compelled for so long to deny any love for the man in her life, Kylie didn't waste any time publicly confirming this fiery affair with Michael. 'Yes, I have seen him,' she revealed to the press soon after arriving in Sydney. 'We've been out on a couple of dates.' Is there any chance of romance in all this, Kylie? 'Could be, might not be,' she laughed. 'He's kind of different from what people would expect him to be like. For instance, I'm sure people look at me and think I'm just two-dimensional and you can't imagine what it would be like to get beyond that. And Michael, he's really impressive. He's really, like, deep sometimes.' Are we talking marriage and kids this time? 'Yeah, well I might have kids without being a wife!'

Kylie was suddenly speaking her mind, her new, open mind, without a script. Her minders went into panic mode. Kylie would have nothing of it. She quickly let everyone know that everything was about to change again. Kylie, she declared for all to hear, was now in the business of doing the unexpected.

'It sounds like I'm a complete hippy but I have found myself more,' was her explanation. 'It's a sense of self and a sense of direction and, because of that, I'm really looking forward to the future.'

Certainly, the initial news of Kylie's new relationship shook her family home. 'When she told me, I was very shocked,' confessed an open-mouthed Dannii. 'I couldn't picture them together. But now that we've met, it's fine.'

Privately, beyond all Michael and Kylie's talk about pop philosophy and life, beyond the world's growing awareness of their fling, there burned an intense passion. Michael regularly boasted to friends that 'Kylie is the best fuck in the world.'

Back on home soil, Michael led Kylie to the dark heart of his rock'n'roll world and introduced her to his nightlife. Kylie immediately moved into Michael's rented apartment high above Sydney's Hyde Park. The sparsely furnished place was constantly buzzing with regular visits from Michael's many friends across Sydney's ultra-cool art, fashion and music cliques.

Kylie loved this life, and felt surprisingly comfortable interacting with people in this hippest of scenes. She felt they respected her. And most did: if Kylie was cool by Michael, then she was cool by everyone else. Kylie loved the idea of being cool.

Kylie and Michael spent much of the following couple of months based in Sydney. Kylie had to briefly dart back to the UK early in December for the London premiere of *The Delinquents* but immediately returned to her new man and home.

At this time, the pair spent many of their afternoons and early evenings over at the INXS studio. Most nights, the socialising wouldn't start until well past midnight. Sometimes they'd catch up with a group of friends back at the apartment for a drink and a spliff. Other nights it would be a band or a nightclub, partying until daylight.

Kylie had never lived this life before. At one point, her family and minders in Melbourne went crazy when they lost all contact with their girl for a week. Perhaps not so coincidentally, it was during these early days in Sydney that Kylie first experimented with drugs.

It took Michael a while to convince Kylie that a bit of dope or an ecstasy tablet wouldn't kill her. Kylie soon relented. The couple became regular early-morning fixtures in a handful of Sydney's trendiest nightclubs. On some outings, Kylie would look worse for wear, stumbling downstairs, crashing out on lounges.

Michael never made a secret of his fondness for drugs. He once quipped that he spent the whole of 1988 with one arm in an eccy jar. Kylie couldn't keep up with that sort of intake, nor did she have any desire to.

'Kylie experimented but not much,' testified one of the couple's friends. 'She had ecstasy a few times. Mainly, she was just having a few drinks. Because she hadn't really been a drinker before. So she'd have a few Fluffy Ducks and she'd be shit-faced.'

Kylie would later have to repeatedly deny widespread rumours that she was rushed to hospital one evening in this period to have her stomach pumped clean of a cocktail of drugs. One version of the story had the incident take place in Melbourne, another in Sydney.

While Terry Blamey insisted to the media that Michael wasn't a drug addict and hadn't introduced Kylie to drugs (Blamey was also claiming that Michael had nothing to do with his client's image change), Kylie foolishly made a roundabout public confession of drug use. 'It can be fun and it can be dangerous,' she told a journalist. 'I'm all for kids not taking drugs. But I don't want to say to them you should never try anything. You have to experience something to have a view on it. Do you know what I'm saying?'

163

Kylie's comments caused a minor political uproar. 'Not only are these comments incorrect,' growled one Australian federal minister, 'but they show a remarkable naivety about the tendency of besotted fans to take everything their idols say at face value.'

'What I was saying was I don't want to preach to children,' Kylie offered in her own defence. 'Most are pretty aware of drugs.' (Several years later, Kylie categorically changed her stance on the matter, stating: 'Some things you can only talk about if you've had experience, but I would condemn drugs now'.)

In the meanwhile, Kylie and Michael's weekends were a totally different scene to their nocturnal escapades. As Greg Perano, an old musician friend of Michael's, put it: 'Michael introduced Kylie to nightclubs and she introduced him to daylight. Michael's never minded going out until four or five in the morning, so she'd do that. But at the same time, he knew he could totally relax with her and go hang in a park with her and do those things that she grew up doing.'

Kylie and Michael often took long rides on the rock star's Harley Davidson motorcycle, stopping wherever for a picnic. Occasionally they'd invite a group of friends along. It was during a quiet stroll through Sydney's Centennial Park a couple of weeks before the Australian premiere of *The Delinquents* that the media reared its ugly head from behind the bushes.

An Australian magazine, *Woman's Day*, published three pages of intimate photos of Kylie and Michael hugging and kissing in the park, Kylie stripped down to her bra. A photographer had sold the pictures to the magazine for $10 000. He then sold them to London's *News of the World* for another $50 000.

The incident caused an immediate international media stir. Some commentators rambled that the photos were a set-up, and so was this whole Kylie-and-Michael thing, for that matter. They labelled it a partnership of convenience, an ingenious promotional ploy, and even suggested that Kylie and her management were probably in for a cut of the cash from the photos. They weren't, but Blamey must have hated the fact that he'd never thought of the idea.

The photos infuriated Kylie and Michael. 'This is all new to me and it's something I've tried to avoid, but I guess I've just been thrown into it,' mumbled the rocker. 'I know all's fair in love and war but when you go off and try to be yourself and it ends up on the front page of the press, it's frightening, knowing your life is under such scrutiny. I don't know why someone should get paid that much just to embarrass us. But if I catch them, they'll know about it. They'll seriously know about it.'

Kylie, of course, was more accustomed to this sort of media

intrusion on her private life, but even she felt that the park photos crossed a line. 'We were mightily pissed off about that because we were having a really idyllic day and then we ended up seeing the guy and we didn't know how long he'd been following us. We knew it was going to happen some time but we just didn't like the idea of some guy making a load of money out of our fame. It's just, you know, a little annoying. It's hard enough to start a romance without the rest of the world watching you.

'On the surface it appears that there's a lot that's known about me,' added Kylie, 'but the beauty of it is that there's a hell of a lot that no one will ever know. I know that no matter what photos they take of me, paparazzi photos through the bathroom window, whatever it might be, they can't really get you. They can't get to your soul.'

Then Kylie and Michael made their dramatic official arrival onto the world stage together at *The Delinquents'* premiere. 'When we arrived, people were saying, "Who is she? She must be famous," smirked Kylie's personal stylist, Nicole Bonython. 'They were just so confused until they saw Michael Hutchence with her.'

It was Bonython who'd bought the wig and organised Kylie's startling look for the pivotal event. 'We thought of doing something different,' she explained.

'I was very careful that night.' Kylie later confessed in reference to her tiny costume. She also described the evening as the highlight of her involvement with the film. 'It was a really fun night.'

After the public proceedings, Kylie and Michael took a group of their closest friends back to their apartment where they saw the sunrise in with cocaine and French champagne.

A few days later, Kylie found herself back in her old world of Melbourne to spend Christmas with her family and prepare for her first all-live concerts. In his New Year's Eve *Review of the Decade* for the BBC, comic Clive James named Kylie 'woman of the decade'.

Kylie's debut gig with a live backing band was scheduled for the Brisbane Entertainment Centre on 3 February 1990. Two more shows would immediately follow, in Sydney and Melbourne. For her whole music career so far, Kylie had largely avoided the issue of performing live, claiming, 'I was determined not to give in to any pressure to perform before I was ready.' It wasn't as if her music needed the extra exposure in any case.

Even though the recent 'Disco in Dreams' tour, which played to 170 000 fans in the UK and grossed an estimated $5 million, provided Kylie with the additional encouragement necessary to give the go-ahead to a full-scale tour, she remained a little apprehensive of what awaited her. 'It will be a great challenge. It is a risk because it's really putting myself out to be either raised up or thrown sticks at, but that's what this whole business is about. It's pretty scary putting yourself out there but you'll never learn if you never take the plunge.'

Kylie's musical tastes had changed dramatically along with everything else during those first few months with Michael. Prince remained Kylie's favourite artist by far but Michael introduced her to the new sounds of contemporaries such as Young MC, De La Soul, Eric B and DJ Jazzy Jeff. These new musical influences, however, wouldn't filter through to Kylie's forthcoming live shows, in which she was constrained to the pure pop ditties of that old Kylie's first two albums. Meanwhile, her latest single, the ballad 'Tears on My Pillow', from *The Delinquents*' soundtrack, gave the singer another number two debut on the English charts.

Terry Blamey set about organising an eight-piece band out of his cabaret contacts in Melbourne. Kylie insisted two of her new friends be included in the line-up – Michael's old musician buddies James Freud, on bass and Greg Perano, on percussion. Perano would later describe the Kylie tour as a military operation. While in Sydney, Kylie and Michael regularly attended gigs by Perano's underground rock band, The Deadly Hume. With Kylie's own band line-up settled, much of January 1990 was spent in Melbourne rehearsing.

Freud was a peculiar choice of bandmate for Kylie, considering she was well aware that only a year earlier he'd growled at a journalist: 'I hate Stock Aitken Waterman. I think they've set popular music back twenty years and they've created the situation where young kids are just buying the rubbish. I'll be glad the day SAW disappear. It's not going to last much longer, it really isn't. That's the only ray of sunshine I can see.' But Freud had said all that before meeting Kylie. If the pop poppet was now Michael's girlfriend, then she was automatically a friend of Freud's.

Kylie's first show turned out to be something of a low-key affair, a warm-up gig, played under the transparent pseudonym of The Singing Budgies, at a Melbourne club called the Cadillac Bar on 29 January. Kylie, along with her band and four dancers, performed thirteen songs in front of 1200 people, including a cover of the Four Tops' 'My Girl'. Scribbled across the top of Kylie's song list were the words: 'Look. Enjoy. Dance.'

A week earlier, Kylie made one of her regular trips to Sydney to visit Michael, this time to help him celebrate his thirtieth birthday. Kylie personally assisted in organising the party, held in an inner-city warehouse and attended by two hundred of Michael's friends. Guests included the other members of INXS, Dannii and American actor Billy Zane.

The evening was an ecstasy-fuelled, blissed-out affair. When it came time to bring out the birthday cake, Kylie carried it into the room held high above her head, a chain of dancing party-goers linked up behind her, others banging out a conga rhythm on empty plastic buckets.

Within a couple of weeks, Kylie had completed her short Australian tour, grossing another $3 million to add to the $14 million she reportedly earned in 1989. The normally cynical local critics seemed surprised by the shows. One who reviewed the official opening night of the tour in Brisbane noted that Kylie had finally proved that she could actually 'sing and she can dance and she can even do both at once very well'. Of her hometown stadium show in Melbourne, another reviewer exuberantly declared that: 'It's time to ditch the snobbery and face facts – the kid's a star.'

'People are starting to come around,' gloated Michael. 'They're saying that she's growing up. I think she's almost becoming hip.'

Despite the prepubescent make-up of her audiences, a hangover from the old Kylie days, the singer was pleased enough with her performances, and immediately announced that she was extending the tour to take in the UK, Europe and Asia through April and May. For the moment, though, it was back to her dream world with Michael in Sydney, where INXS continued its work on *X*.

During these months in Sydney, Kylie and Michael occasionally ducked off to get a few days alone. There were trips to Hong Kong, a holiday on Great Keppel Island, off the north-eastern Australian coast; even weekends spent in the solitude of cheap beachside motels in Bondi, only a few kilometres from the couple's city apartment. Kylie and Michael took several trips away in the weeks following Kylie's Australian tour. They already knew they'd be seeing little of each other in the months to come.

By mid-March 1990, Kylie was sharing a rented apartment with Terry Blamey in Hollywood. The two had arrived in LA so that Kylie could work with some different music producers and Blamey could search out some more film work.

Kylie's primary reason for being in the USA was to work with a handful of high-profile American producers. She enlisted the services of Stephen Bray (who'd co-written the Madonna monster hits 'Into the Groove' and 'Express Yourself'), Paula Abdul producer Keith Cohen, and Martika producer Michael Jay.

Four of the songs from the LA sessions, all co-written by Kylie, would make it on to her next album, *Rhythm of Love*. 'The best way to describe my American work,' explained Kylie, 'is as a collaboration. That's something I hadn't done before and it was great. I learnt a lot from those guys and they were interested in what I had to say. With SAW songs, I heard them the day I recorded them, sometimes two songs in a day. I have to be careful not to make PWL [Peter Waterman Limited] sound like an absolute nightmare but to work on a song, demo it and live with it for a while is bliss, and a much longer process than what I'm used to.'

Kylie dedicated one of the songs, 'Count the Days', to Michael. 'That's about being away from each other because it's obviously difficult for us to match up – we're both so busy.'

Michael had already written one for Kylie – 'Suicide Blonde'. Years later, Michael recalled the inspiration for the song, which would top charts around the world by the end of 1990: 'Kylie dyed her hair this colour she called suicide blonde. She said, "I'm going to go suicide blonde today." I think she was thinking of people like Marilyn Monroe and I thought it was a good name, especially as Madonna was big at the time.'

Soon after returning home to Australia in April, Kylie was off again, this time to the UK to start the European leg of her 'Enjoy Yourself' tour. The month-long run of shows, which included an appearance at the John Lennon Memorial Concert in Liverpool at the start of May, was gruelling. A sell-out throughout England, the tour ran into poor attendances on the Continent. That was Kylie's fault. It had been a year since she last did any promotion in Europe. She detested talking to its media, especially the Germans.

'It just wasn't a lot of fun,' recalled bassist James Freud. 'The band was treated pretty scummy. There wasn't much contact with Kylie. She was the boss. Every night we'd come off stage and go back to the hotel and there'd be a piano in the bar and Adrian

[Scott, the tour's musical director] would sit there and play and all the singers would stand around and sing "The Greatest Love of All".'

Asia was a different story to Europe. Asia still loved Kylie. The tour wound up on a high note with a chaotic show in Bangkok late in May. At the end-of-tour party, which doubled as Kylie's twenty-second birthday, Michael presented her with a huge diamond-encrusted ring. Prior to catching up in Hong Kong a week earlier, Kylie and Michael hadn't seen each other for a month.

Tour's end coincided with Kylie filming an advert for Coca-Cola and the release of her latest single, 'Better the Devil You Know'. The song was the first sample of music from the new-generation Kylie, and the high-energy dance track sounded nothing like the old stuff.

By this stage, Kylie was running her show. Over the course of the last six months, she'd personally grasped control of every aspect of her image, from photos to the production of her video-clips. SAW didn't want any of this to happen, but what could they do? Kylie was the biggest and most enduring star they had. She now got whatever she asked for, regardless of the potential damage to her career.

What's more, Kylie even had the audacity to demand that SAW produce the type of songs that she wanted or she wouldn't sing them anymore. From here on, Kylie had final veto on which tracks ended up on her albums.

'Better the Devil You Know' caused the first drama in this new power structure. Kylie hated the original mix of the song and forced SAW to do it again. At the same time, SAW hated the feedback they were getting about the clip Kylie was filming in Melbourne. 'I had people saying, "Oh, you're stupid, you shouldn't do that",' Kylie later relayed. 'Generally everyone was freaking out.

It's like they only want to see you in the same way that they've always known you.'

The clip Kylie finally presented SAW with for 'Better the Devil You Know' was a radical departure from her previous body of work. The video featured a skimpily clad, perfectly toned Kylie dancing madly, behaving like a wild animal, nestling herself in the arms of a naked black man twice her size. It made for a mind-boggling artistic leap from the clip for 'Hand on Your Heart' only a year earlier. This particular performance would go a long way towards earning Kylie some of the street-cred she now desperately desired, and started making her hip in the world's hippest dance clubs.

Despite all of SAW's protestations and proclamations of doom, the single debuted at number five on the UK charts, soon peaking at number two. Kylie's actions had been vindicated by her public.

Kylie and Michael moved to London in June 1990. INXS was scheduled to mix its *X* album and Kylie had to finish recording *Rhythm of Love*. Once those tasks were completed, Kylie and Michael took off for an extended holiday in Europe, spending two weeks in Italy. On their way home, the pair picked up a $480 000 four-bedroom villa in the south of France.

Kylie and Michael spent much of the next few months between their pads in France, Hong Kong and Sydney. Come September, Michael was back in London preparing for the release of *X* and another major international tour. Kylie hung around when she could and caught as many shows as her promotional schedule would allow.

By the end of 1990, Kylie had released her third album, *Rhythm of Love* (which, surprisingly, only peaked at number nine on the UK charts and number ten in Australia), released another successful single ('Step Back in Time', which peaked at number four in the UK, Kylie's eleventh straight hit there), and was again holidaying with Michael in London and in the south of France.

It had been a good year for Kylie, there was no doubt about it. 'I'm a lot happier than I used to be,' Kylie said towards the end of 1990. 'I'm more calm and not so strung-out. And not so worried and not so scared about things. I'm sure most people who are my age go through the same things.

'The last year has been so fulfilling and personally great, not just workwise. Michael is another reason the last year has been incredible, he's expanded my world a little further. He's very knowledgeable and I learn a lot from him but it's not a teacher/student thing. He affects me, that's why we have a relationship, and I'm sure he learns from me too.

'People are taking me a lot more seriously now. There's been a general change towards me everywhere and it's definitely for the better. People are listening now and, I don't know, it's nice. I feel more solid, I feel like I've finally made it. For a one-hit wonder, I've been here for a long time.'

Kylie was now also being frank about her constantly deteriorating relationship with SAW. 'I think they lost the plot for a while and I told them that. Four years ago when they were really big, they had new sounds and they were ahead of their time. They've been doing so many songs and I don't know how long they can keep doing it for.

'People get too jaded. They find a formula that works and stick to it. I can't do that. I've played safe for too long.'

Did Kylie have any idea what shape future changes might take? 'At the moment, my image is very much a girl-woman,' she grinned. 'I hope I can be like that forever.'

Kylie's stylist Nicole Bonython was more deadpan in her prediction of possible trends. 'I think we'll just continue in the sex vein,' she explained. 'That's how Kylie feels at the moment and it suits her. Until the next change, that is.'

Kylie and Michael's blissful romance wouldn't see out another year. In fact, it barely survived the first few months of 1991. Following their month-long vacation in Europe over Christmas, the first festive season Kylie had ever spent away from her family, Michael took off to begin the American leg of the 'X' tour. Kylie came back home to start rehearsals for her 'Rhythm of Love' tour, scheduled to start in Perth on 13 February.

Kylie and Michael only saw each other again at Kylie's Sydney show late in February. And that's where the relationship collapsed. Kylie had got wind of the fact that Michael wasn't being faithful to her while on the road. As one of Michael's entourage attested, 'Michael fucked around, took in arty types in every city. He had a particular fondness for having sex with two girls at once.'

These rumours broke Kylie's heart. When she confronted Michael with them in Sydney, he didn't deny anything. And that was the end of that.

'He's shocking,' offered one of Michael's mates. 'He's hopeless. He has no control. He's addicted to casual sex. He's been doing it for so long that it's a way of life. That's what broke them up. Kylie wouldn't wear it.'

Michael immediately took off for London again, leaving behind a devastated Kylie. 'I was so hurt when we broke up because I was very much in love with him,' Kylie later confessed. 'I spent a good part of the time crying my heart out. There were days when I just wanted to stay in bed.'

Kylie and Michael didn't talk again for ages. Within months of their break-up, Michael was publicly gallivanting around with a new girl, the nineteen-year-old supermodel Helena Christensen. That relationship was doomed to meet a similar fate.

By the end of 1991, Kylie and Michael were friends again, Kylie often popping up backstage at INXS shows around the globe. Years later, in 1994, bemused guests at an after-show INXS party watched on as Kylie and Michael disappeared together into a toilet cubicle for nearly an hour.

Despite the heartache, it didn't take Kylie long to get over Michael. Within a few months she had her own new boy and was ready to start the next phase of her unpredictable life. From here on, nothing and no one could keep Kylie down for long.

KYLIE FINALLY FINDS HERSELF IN THE ARMS

OF HER TRUE PRINCE.

RADICAL DIVA

the complete star

It's early May 1994, and Kylie, only weeks away from her twenty-sixth birthday, is slow-dancing cheek-to-cheek with the American artist presently known as Prince. The setting is the after-show party to the annual World Music Awards in Monte Carlo. Kylie has been a regular guest at the awards for several years now. The soundtrack to this scene is Prince's own current global hit, 'The Most Beautiful Girl in the World'.

The similarly height-impaired Prince has forever been like a god to Kylie. He is her only idol. She has worshipped him for as long as she can remember. At the peak of her global popularity in 1989, the still girlish Kylie innocently confided to a fashion reporter that, 'The day I meet Prince, my life will be complete. I think we'd make a great pair,' she giggled. 'He's an interesting person and the only artist who I really admire as a fan. He's so outrageous and different. It's funny – he revolts people but others think he's sex on a stick.'

Within a year of those comments, Michael Hutchence had introduced Kylie to the concept of becoming an artist herself, and suddenly a doorway to meeting Prince presented itself. Kylie started sending out personal invitations.

'I'd love to work with him,' she told the media when rumours arose that Prince had attended one of her concerts in London. 'He's my all-time hero. [But] it's difficult getting through to him through his people,' she complained. 'I'd really love to work with him, you know, but maybe this wasn't the right time. I want to take things step by step.

'If Prince wanted to work with me, he'd obviously want to put his brilliance into what I do, and God, I'd want that too. You think I'm going to say no?'

It would take a couple more years for one of Kylie's missiles to hit its target. It eventually did so through an unlikely route. By pure coincidence, Prince's management hired their security men and chauffeurs for an English tour late in 1992 from the same firm used by Kylie Inc.

When Prince arrived in town, a couple of drivers exchanged words and the message got back to Kylie that His Majesty requested an audience with her backstage after his London show. Of course, Kylie was there in a flash. Prince told her to drop by his London studio some time over the next few days.

Kylie promptly took up the invitation and immediately felt like she'd made a mistake. 'There were a few jokes flying around,' Kylie later recalled. "Where do you want your mic set up? Where are your lyrics? Come on!" I don't think he knew much [about me], or at least he didn't let on. But he did mention one quote that I said some time back, about him being sex on a stick. I think I feigned ignorance, as if I didn't know what he was talking about. Which he probably saw straight through.'

Prince told Kylie she should drop over to his place in Minneapolis next time she was in America. A few months later, Kylie popped up on his doorstep. This time she came prepared for the meeting, with a set of lyrics for a song called 'Baby Doll'.

Prince was impressed, and immediately sat down and wrote some music for the words. Kylie stayed on at Prince's Paisley Park for a couple of days. She spent her afternoons watching her idol work in the studio, the evenings relaxing with him, playing pool and table tennis. 'I hung out there for a while and got to know something of Prince and he is a fairly reserved character. What I got to know about him I liked and he's fun. He's a little weird but I'd be disappointed if he wasn't.'

Kylie would later swear the two of them never got intimate, not that Prince wasn't in for a bit of fun. 'I think he's always a bit on the fresh side. But who wants to be on that list? You stop and think, Hang on, I wonder how many other girls have been lured to Minneapolis? If that's what he enjoys, fine, but I'm interested in him and his music, nothing else.

'I think he has some interest in what I'm doing. We'll see what happens in time. There's plenty of time, plenty of time.'

The two artists had kept in phone contact, and now, only another year on, Kylie and Prince are dancing together centre-stage in front of the rest of the world's music glitterati. Included in the crowd at the post-World Music Awards party are Michael Hutchence and Helena Christensen. They all watch on as Kylie's fantasy is realised – to be Prince's peer.

179

The world press immediately dived on this most high-profile display of affection between Kylie and Prince, insisting it was proof of a long-running affair. As Kylie started her twenty-sixth year at the end of May 1994, there were countless other tales of romantic dalliances being flung around the globe's media. There were stories that Kylie was preparing to marry Julian Lennon. The pair had only ever met once, in an LA club a couple of years earlier.

There were also rumours about Kylie and other stars. Her old friend in New York, Lenny Kravitz. The singer of The Lemonheads, Evan Dando.

There was some substance to the story about Dando. During a trip back to Melbourne, the two pop stars met up in a city club, kissed openly and then disappeared into a toilet together for an hour. 'We hung out for a couple of nights,' Kylie later confessed,

the complete star

'so at least there's a reason for stories that we're boyfriend and girlfriend. Which we're not.'

Indeed, Kylie hadn't had a boyfriend since her on-again, off-again relationship with South African Zane O'Donnell finally dissolved late in 1993, when the former model went off to become a born-again Christian. For the first time since she was a teenager, Kylie didn't have a man in her life. And she was happy about the situation. 'For now I'm on the single road again, which is a breath of fresh air.'

After Michael, Kylie went a bit crazy.

Based back in London after the end of her tour through Australia and Asia early in 1991, Kylie immersed herself in the city's nightlife, Zane constantly by her side. Kylie had first met Zane late in 1990 on the set of her 'What Do I Have to Do?' video-clip in London. Kylie was still going out with Michael at the time. As soon as Michael was gone, Zane – who'd recently walked out on his wife and child – was there.

'I was out of control for a while,' Kylie would later admit. 'I was rebelling against everything I couldn't do before. I had to get it out of my system. I was rebelling against being labelled a good girl all the time.'

Through the social contacts Michael had introduced her to, Kylie found herself a whole new crowd. 'I guess most of the people I spend my time with are in the fashion and photography circles rather than the music,' explained Kylie. 'Although these people are very passionate and hip about their music.

'I was lucky. I met up with some people who opened me up to just the right circles. They're fantastic to be with. They don't have dollar signs in their eyes. Some of them are strange but it's a lot of fun to figure them out. I have a great time when I go out. I relax.'

In October of 1991, Kylie embarked on her final tour, this time through Europe. The reviews in London for her new raunchy show were harsher than ever. 'She can loll about in a leather fig-leaf and sing about pumping it up all night long but Kylie is half a pint of semi-skimmed milk and she always will be,' wrote one newspaper. 'It is difficult to adequately describe the kind of numbness that begins to overcome you as you enter the seventeenth successive number,' offered another.

'If I expected anything better from the tabloids I'd be pretty silly, wouldn't I?' was Kylie's dismissive reply.

It was the costumes for the tour that caused the most controversy. Conceived by the English designer John Galliano, the set featured a G-string off-set by a frilly bra, suspenders and fishnets. Another piece was a black vinyl corset. It was a long way from the little suit and baggy cap emblazoned with an Australian flag from Kylie's first tour.

'I wanted something that was outrageous, something that was me and something that was comfortable to move around on stage in,' said Kylie. 'What he [Galliano] came up with was so perfect it was frightening. So then I thought, Okay, I'm going to have to search my confidence to pull this one off. I never thought, Oh no, this is so over the top, because I had said that I wanted something outrageous and something that people would remember for quite some time.'

The costumes intensified the by-now common attacks from unfriendly observers that this new 'SexKylie' was simply trying to rip off Madonna. Kylie had brought it on herself. Since the early days of her singing career, Kylie constantly repeated how Madonna, the most famous female entertainer of her generation, was the kind of artist she wanted to become. Kylie had even used Madonna's old producer and songwriter on the *Rhythm of Love* album. But now Kylie found herself constantly defending accusations of imitation.

'Madonna has definitely influenced me,' explained Kylie, 'as have lots of other people, men and women. I would say Madonna influences me generally rather than specifically. She seems to be a very strong woman, continually breaking new ground. I am certainly not trying to imitate Madonna. I'm continuing to develop my own style.'

Kylie's European tour coincided with the release of her final studio album through the PWL label. Matt Aitken had left the company early in 1991. Under the singer's insistence, half the songs on *Let's Get to It* were co-written by Kylie and Mike Stock.

Stock didn't enjoy the process. 'To sit with Kylie there with *Let's Get to It* and have to work through the process of writing with her, it was just an embarrassing situation for me,' he recalled. 'I found that difficult with Kylie. Not impossible but difficult.

'Normally I'd have a clear idea for a song before she'd come. Obviously, she had a busy schedule so she wasn't there every day. Then she'd come and sit down and we'd work through the lyric and the finer points. And she had a pad with ideas written down. Matt and I never kept one of those.'

Kylie was under no obligation to make her fourth record for PWL, and it would have been easy to slip out of her contract early. But Blamey figured a new album would be a good money-spinner during the tour, so an album was compiled out of unused tracks and the new Stock/Kylie compositions.

Kylie insisted that the R&B-flavoured *Let's Get to It* was her favourite recording so far. The media's reaction gave some indication of how much things had changed over the two previous years. The readers of *Smash Hits* magazine in England now voted Kylie the worst female singer of the year. Alternatively, the country's hip music papers, which had slung Kylie grief for so long, had now changed their tune. *Melody Maker* called *Let's Get to It*

'Great. More than great. Exceptional. Album of the week, of the month even.' *NME* said Kylie was 'a genius of pop'.

But by Kylie's standards, the record proved to be a commercial flop. In the UK, it only reached number fifteen on the charts. In Australia, it got to seventeen. Its single, 'Word is Out', also did badly. It was the first song not to make the top ten in the UK. And by this stage, in every other market in the world, Kylie was virtually a has-been. It had already been a couple of years since Kylie refused to take on any more publicity treks through Europe and her name rarely appeared on the music charts anywhere across the Continent again.

Kylie saw out much of 1992 enjoying a life liberated of work obligations. She spent much of the year away from the limelight, living in her new apartment in Paris with Zane. By the end of 1992, the pair was back in London. Kylie had bought a sparse, sixth-floor apartment for half a million pounds in the trendy inner-city suburb of Chelsea. She shared it with Zane until the end of 1993. When Zane walked out, Kylie would share the place with two friends: first, an Australian singer called Nicki Love, and then, later, her new personal assistant, Charlene Fenn, an old co-star from the *Neighbours* days.

Towards the end of 1992, PWL released its final Kylie album – her *Greatest Hits*. The record and accompanying video, featuring Kylie's unbroken string of eighteen UK top 20 singles along with two new recordings, made for an astonishing document of the last five insane years.

The album was also unquestionably Kylie's best record thus far. After all, it was Kylie's singles and their videos that were the obvious highlights of her musical career. Each of Kylie's other albums suffered from an abundance of fillers – Hit Factory cuttings that could have just as easily landed on the studio floor, or on an album from one of PWL's many other artists.

But Kylie's *Greatest Hits* was flawless – a non-stop stream of classic pop, each track a certified hit. Fittingly, the collection put Kylie back on top of the English charts.

In April 1993, Kylie signed a new multimillion-dollar record deal with the hip English dance music label deConstruction. They promised Kylie that she could do anything that she wanted.

'deConstruction have a brilliant reputation to uphold,' offered Kylie, 'so I'm kind of relying on their reputation rather than my own. There were two options. Either we could make another pop record or we could throw me into the field and just try anything. We chose the latter.'

'Kylie is regarded as a trashy disco singer,' offered Pete Hatfield, co-founder of deConstruction. 'We regard her as a potential radical dance diva.'

'We just think she's a complete star,' enthused his partner Keith Blackhurst. 'She's almost like a diva. We just thought the opportunity to work with Kylie, who'd obviously grown up, was an opportunity to have a star, in the true sense of the word, working with us and our team of creative people.'

The deConstruction team included the label's already proven modern hit-makers, production duo Brothers in Rhythm. 'When she first came into the studio, her voice was the sound of PWL,' said the Brothers' Steve Anderson. 'It had that nasal quality to it, the horrible Kylie Minogue voice that graced a great many records. Throughout the course of recording the album, she gained confidence in her vocals and surprised herself with what she could do.'

In September 1994, a year and a half after signing to de-Construction, the first fruit of the new relationship, a single called 'Confide in Me', was released. It had been twenty-one months since Kylie's last single. Backed by a 32-piece orchestra,

Kylie sounded angelic, nothing like a PWL artist. The single shot to number two on the English charts and number one in Australia.

Kylie Minogue, the singer's first full new studio album in three years, followed a month later. It was accompanied by a limited-edition coffee/table book exhibiting Kylie in various states of undress. The obvious similarity in theme to Madonna's highly publicised *Sex* book from a few years earlier immediately rekindled those rip-off slurs. The same month, Kylie appeared nude – all her rude bits strategically out of view – on the cover of a British magazine, *Sky*.

Meanwhile, the album's songwriting credits included the likes of the Brothers in Rhythm duo, Jimmy Harry (the American producer of drag-queen star, RuPaul) and the Pet Shop Boys. The Boys' Chris Lowe had long heralded Kylie as the greatest pop artist of her era.

Noticeably missing from the list was Kylie's own name; she only shared a split credit on one song, 'Automatic Love'. 'I enjoy writing but it's not something that I have to do when there are brilliant writers around,' was Kylie's reasoning. 'I would never choose a song that I had written above another song because I had done it. The best song wins.' Indeed, although Kylie had spent much of her time in the lead-up to recording the album collaborating on songs with a variety of artists in both the UK and USA, the team at deConstruction convinced her that none of those songs was really worthy of inclusion. Kylie's desire to become recognised as a songwriter would have to wait a bit longer.

Another brewing frustration for Kylie was America. As with her previous two studio albums, the deConstruction album never ended up getting a widespread release there. Through her new label, Kylie had scored a fresh deal in the USA with Imago Records but internal turmoil in the company saw the album dropped from its major release schedule.

Again the United States eluded her. To American record buyers, Kylie remained a one-hit wonder, that weird little bright thing who covered 'Locomotion' back in 1988.

Kylie's career in the USA never recovered from Geffen Records' sudden loss of interest in her following the release of her second album, *Enjoy Yourself*. By that stage, Geffen had created its own all-American girl-next-door superstar, a seventeen-year-old called Tiffany who'd already proven herself with a worldwide hit, 'I Think We're Alone Now'. Geffen felt it no longer needed to import that sort of product. Soon, its office even stopped bothering to return PWL's calls.

There was one strand of American culture that proved an exception to the nation's general disinterest in Kylie, a subculture that worshipped her with a passion to match that of all those kids around the world back in the late eighties – the gay community.

Like other gay clubbers around the globe, American gays adopted Kylie as an iconic diva. Her music and all its kitsch trimmings elevated Kylie to the ranks of Judy Garland, Liza Minnelli, Eartha Kitt and Barbra Streisand in their eyes.

Kylie's cult following among gays dated as far back as her first worldwide hit, 'I Should be so Lucky', in 1988. While the song was number one in Australia, a club in Melbourne staged a Kylie revue with drag queens sending up her hit. Her minders at the time didn't bring this sideshow to Kylie's attention, fearing the naive singer wouldn't quite know how to deal with the tribute.

But by 1993, following Jason's 'Queer as Fuck' run-in with *The Face* magazine, Kylie's global gay following had grown so large and vocal that the singer went out of her way to publicly acknowledge its existence. In the middle of the year, by which time drag Kylie impersonators had popped up in cities everywhere, Kylie headlined a show at London's Bang Club, which was the culmination to Gay Pride Day. 'I'm very thankful for your continued support,' she told the 1500 revellers.

Suddenly, gay magazines in the UK and Australia were getting calls from Terry Blamey's office with offers of exclusive Kylie interviews. Kylie told one such magazine that she couldn't remember when she first noticed her gay audience. 'But I remember I was blown away when I heard about the Kylie Show,' she said.

Kylie didn't get to see one of those Kylie shows until she was back in Melbourne at the end of 1993 to visit her family for Christmas. 'A friend of mine did me a favour so I more or less owed him one and I said, "I tell you what, I'll come to Three Faces [the city's premier gay nightclub] with you, let them know and see if they'll do a show for me", because I'd never seen anyone impersonating me.

187

'I was screaming my head off. They wore two of my favourite oufits – one was the noughts-and-crosses dress I wore years ago to *The Delinquents* premiere with Michael and the other one was the ostrich-feather hotpants with the pink chequered bra from the video for "Shocked". I laughed and laughed and laughed.

'One of them in particular, Millie Minogue, looked so much more like me than I did because I was kind of on the natural side. She was, you know, working everything. I felt like I paled in comparison.'

The following year, in the middle of 1994, Kylie made a head-lining appearance at another major gay celebration, this time in front of 20 000 ecstasy-fuelled punters at the party following Sydney's annual Gay and Lesbian Mardi Gras parade. Wearing a tiny pink tutu and surrounded by a troupe of similarly dressed drag queens, Kylie performed only one song.

'The song which I did, which was "What Do I Have to Do?", is probably fourth on my list of my favourite ones to do if I'm just to do one song,' Kylie explained afterwards. 'But the problem was they'd already done the other ones. Apparently there'd been forty Kylies doing "Better the Devil You Know".

'It was quite moving. I wish I could have stayed and enjoyed the party and to blend in and feel like part of the crowd, which I tried to do but it wasn't really working. I felt very touched at having such an appreciative crowd and just to be able to have the opportunity to say thank you because I've had a lot of support from the gay community.'

It's January 1994 and Kylie, wearing a very conservative black dress with white embroidery, her hair back to the natural, long blonde curls of old, finds herself in the middle of a very heterosexual affair. Finally a Minogue wedding. Dannii's.

Kylie plays the bridesmaid as her little sister takes actor Julian McMahon, the son of a former Australian Prime Minister, as her husband. 'I was grinning like a Cheshire cat,' Kylie said afterwards. 'I had sore cheeks I was so happy for them.' Kylie attended the wedding alone, her long-term relationship with Zane O'Donnell having collapsed for a final time a few months earlier.

At the wedding reception, the Minogue sisters grabbed hold of centre stage for a rendition of 'We are Family' backed by the house band. Lady Sonia McMahon, Julian's mother and former Australian first lady, was not amused. She considered the Minogue clan as a lower caste. Meanwhile, Terry Blamey had already sewn up a deal to sell the photos from the event exclusively to an Australian women's magazine.

Within a year, Dannii and Julian's marriage was in tatters. After only three weeks together, Julian was pursuing his acting career in New York while Dannii did television work in the UK. The split was rumoured to have come when Dannii caught Julian in bed with one of his co-stars from the American television soap, *Another World*.

'That was my first failure and there'll be lots to come,' Dannii offered by way of a post-mortem. 'Obviously, when you are walking down the aisle you want it to work and you want it to be for the rest of your life. For that not to happen, it's a failure. It doesn't mean that I wouldn't get married again.'

It didn't deter Kylie from her long-held family aspirations either. 'I know that I will have a family,' Kylie constantly reiterated. 'That's one of the things I know for sure about the future.'

In late January 1995, Kylie, dressed casually in white summer pants, sandals and a yellow T-shirt featuring a panda, arrives in a Melbourne studio to perform a duet with the city's only other international musical icon, Nick Cave. It's a bizarre pairing, ranking right up there with the shock value of the Kylie-and-Michael union.

Terry Blamey is in tow, carrying with him a short contract for everyone involved to sign. It forbids anyone to talk to the press about the session until he approves the recording, and it guarantees the song won't be heard outside the studio unless everyone is happy with the results.

Blamey didn't want this recording to happen. He was infuriated when he found out that Kylie was delivered a tape from Cave without his authorisation, and he exploded at the record-company employee who'd acted as the go-between.

Like Kylie, Nick Cave was back in Melbourne to spend Christmas with his mother. Through one of the people at Mushroom Records, the label that handles both artists' releases in Australia, he had an audio cassette delivered to Kylie with a note that read: 'Here's a demo. Love to do it with you. Give me a call.'

On the tape was a rough version of a song Cave had written

specifically with Kylie in mind called 'Where the Wild Roses Grow'. A slow, morose waltz, it set Kylie in the character of Eliza Day, a chaste and love-struck beauty who gets bashed to death by her lover.

Cave had gone public about his desire to record with Kylie years before. During his 1992 European tour, a travel bag emblazoned with her name had been his constant companion and the focal point of many of his publicity photos. When the bag was eventually stolen, it was all Cave could talk about in interviews.

Despite his sincerity, many in the international music press interpreted Cave's apparent obsession with Kylie as just another example of his warped humour. After all, even though the two artists grew up within a ten-minute drive of each other in Melbourne, their paths to fame and what each represented to popular culture couldn't have been more extreme. While Kylie had been labelled 'The Singing Budgie', Nick was nicknamed 'The King of Goth'. When Kylie was farewelling the cast of wholesome *Neighbours* back in 1988, Cave was in rehab kicking a smack habit. To those rock'n'roll magazines that had portrayed Kylie as the ultimate pop puppet, Cave was a dark, tortured musical genius.

After the eventual release of 'Where the Wild Roses Grow', Cave again tried to earnestly explain that he had wanted to do a song with Kylie from the first moment he saw her. 'I've known her stuff since she started,' he said, 'and I was always struck by how uncynical she seemed to be about things. Apart from just her basic charm and so forth, she seemed very open and honest. I have written several songs for her over the years but none of them seemed quite right. Until now. I think Kylie is as burdened by her image as I am and I think I recognise and sympathise with that.'

Kylie admitted she'd been aware of Cave's constant attention from afar. 'I had read in a couple of his interviews kind words about me,' she said, 'and he had a little Kylie tour bag which was so touching. I'd also heard through Michael Hutchence that he wanted to work with me. I was always open to the idea but never actively pursued it. I figured it would just come around.'

Unbeknown to Kylie, Cave's management had contacted hers as far back as 1989 to air the idea of a collaboration. But Blamey, believing such a project would leave Kylie looking like an idiot, refused to let it go any further, not even bothering to tell her about it.

This time around, one of Cave's bandmates, bassist Mick Harvey, decided he'd try the direct approach. He phoned Michael Hutchence to ask the singer if he knew where his old girlfriend could be found. Coincidentally, Kylie was right there, sitting next to Hutchence. She got on the phone and told Harvey she loved the idea of working with Cave.

When 'Where the Wild Roses Grow' arrived on her doorstep a fortnight later, Kylie immediately agreed with the choice of song, leaving a message for Cave the next day to tell him so. 'I was more than happy to do it,' she enthused. 'I was very intrigued and excited. So we arranged it. The funniest part was we were both leaving messages with each other's mothers. "Hi, is Nick there? Oh, okay, can you get him to call me at home?" And then he would call my mother and leave a message with her. I thought that was beautiful.'

'No one knew what to expect,' said the song's producer, Victor Van Vugt, 'but as soon as Kylie walked in, she made everyone feel so comfortable. Her manager certainly had a few worries but Kylie came in, sat on the couch with the band – they were all there in their suits – and they had a laugh. After about half an hour of chatting, she went up to sing. As soon as she went into the recording room, everyone went for their cigarettes and she was like, "Oh, yeah, you're all lighting up now that I've left the room." Which was true.'

191

Kylie sang her part half a dozen times and the eventual version would feature a compilation of three of her takes. 'She'd obviously been practising and rehearsing,' said Van Vugt. 'She just knew exactly how to sing it. She's a much better singer and a lot more musical than you'd probably expect. The first take was really good and it improved. And she had ideas about singing slightly behind the beat to make it a bit more intense. Certainly a trained singer.'

The whole session ended up lasting less than two hours. Nevertheless, Cave would later refer to it as 'a deeply spiritual experience'. He added that 'it was amazing working with her. All my dreams came true. She was great.'

Kylie was similarly impressed. 'It's a beautiful song,' she said. 'And he's very charming and charismatic. It was an experience to work with him but, also, the way he made me perform was different to anything I've done. It's a really different vocal. You probably wouldn't know it was me at all. I'm really glad it's happened.'

Indeed, Cave made Kylie sound nothing like Kylie. Singing in a lower register than usual, and with her vocal left free of studio effects, her breathy voice trembles and gives life to the melodramatic notion of her character speaking from the grave.

When the single version of 'Where the Wild Roses Grow' was released in October, it reached number two on the Australian charts, selling over 50 000 copies.

Kylie and Cave's paths would cross several times throughout the remainder of the year. At the end of March, she again visited Cave in the studio, this time in London, to sing a few lines on another track for his *Murder Ballads* album, a cover version of Bob Dylan's 'Death is Not the End'. Then there was the filming of the video-clip for 'Wild Roses', which had Kylie dressed in a skimpy white satin number and spending most of her on-screen time playing a corpse lying in a river. At separate points, a snake and

Cave's hands slither over her body, prompting London's *Daily Mirror* to exclaim: 'Kylie Strips in Satan Video – She's Fondled by Singer Cave'.

Later in the year, Kylie invited Cave to join her on stage at a couple of British summer music festivals where she was appearing with other acts from her record label, deConstruction. Kylie and Cave performed their duet at the Feile festival in Cork and in front of 30 000 people at the T in the Park festival in Glasgow. When they later sat down to interview each other for an article in an Australian newspaper, Cave told Kylie that, 'When I got up and sang that song with you, it was possibly the most terrifying time I've ever been on stage in my life. I've had people try to hit me over the head with iron bars and urinate on me, but nothing has made me as uncomfortable as singing to that pocket of Kylie Minogue purists at the front who were shaking their fingers whenever I touched you or held your hands, defiling your sacredness.'

Cave also confessed to Kylie that he'd had an erotic dream about her the night before their interview. In the dream, as Cave described it, he pulled his hands out of his pockets and found his fingers pierced by fish hooks. Suddenly, they were being tugged from behind him. He turned and there was Kylie pulling at them. 'Oh, I'm so pleased,' was Kylie's reaction.

'Nick's got a huge crush on her,' merrily observed Cave's long-time associate and friend, Tony Cohen. 'He probably thought doing the duet was the best way to meet her. He did a great drawing for me of himself relaxing at home, having a pull over a picture of Kylie, which is quite funny.'

Regardless of Cave's original motivation, his association with Kylie helped redefine her public and artistic persona. Long hailed as a darling of the dance and pop crowds, she'd always struggled to gain credibility in traditional rock circles. Hutchence had helped her somewhat on that front. But now, with such an overt pledge of admiration from an indie rock god of the stature of Nick Cave, even Kylie's most savage critics would have to reassess their prejudices towards her.

For her part, Kylie – as she'd done many times before – was able to capitalise on this opportunity that had presented itself to her. With typical finesse and unpretentiousness, she floated into a foreign subculture and, by inventing a new version of herself, claimed her own space. Of greater enduring interest were Kylie's performances in both the song and video, each suggesting there were aspects of her artistic abilities that remained untapped.

Kylie started out 1995 in a very different world. Dressed in white, with the sequins on her see-through T-shirt exclaiming '1995', she saw the new year in on stage in a Sydney dance club in front of some five thousand revellers. Singing live to back-up tapes, she gave a forty-minute performance supported by a troupe of her own dancers and a posse of drag queens. Looking on from the audience was the whole Minogue clan. Kylie would stay on in town for the next three months.

Since winding up her second world tour at the end of 1991, Kylie's only live performances had been a handful of unannounced gigs similar to this. While she once played to stadiums full of screaming kids, she now preferred the intimacy and hysteria of jumping up at dance parties and delivering short, one-off shows whenever she got the urge. This was deConstruction's Radical Dance Diva Kylie – the high-energy, euphoric, elusive gay icon.

A couple of weeks after the recording session for 'Wild Roses', Kylie found herself in the middle of another unlikely project. At a dinner party one evening soon after she'd arrived home, a girlfriend handed her a script for a short film entitled *Hayride to Hell*.

Kylie had only recently got back into acting. She'd been in Queensland in 1994 to work on her first Hollywood-funded project, the $44 million film adaptation of the popular video-arcade game, *Street Fighter*. It was her first acting role since 1989's *The Delinquents*.

Street Fighter's director, Steven de Souza, had spotted a photo of Kylie on the cover of an Australian magazine under the heading 'The 30 Most Beautiful People in the World'. He immediately decided he wanted Kylie to play the character of Cammy, a British intelligence officer and personal assistant to the story's hero, Colonel Guile, played by Belgian-born action-man Jean-Claude Van Damme.

Kylie underwent a stringent fitness campaign in preparation for the role, taking on martial arts and pumping iron. But her screen-time in the final product was limited to a handful of forgettable scenes. So even though *Street Fighter* proved a considerable commercial success in America, grossing $70 million in box-office receipts, it did virtually nothing to raise Kylie's profile in that market. Again, that goal would have to be put aside for later.

Hayride to Hell was about as far removed from *Street Fighter* as Hollywood is to Sydney. A low-budget, eleven-minute art-house flick, it would require only one week's work from Kylie. Having read the script and taken a liking to the psychotic character she'd have to portray, Kylie was in. 'Investment and return-wise, it seemed like a great thing to do,' assessed the actress.

Set in the backstreets of the Sydney suburb of Darlinghurst, *Hayride to Hell* opens with Kylie's nameless and frenetic character jumping into the car of a stranger, George Table, played by local actor Richard Roxburgh. Sporting a short, jet-black hair-do and, once again, looking nothing like Kylie, the junkie-like character tells the driver she's a diabetic, demands to be taken to her apartment, and then faints.

When she doesn't re-emerge from the building, Table goes in search of her, eventually finding her unconscious in an elevator.

She comes to and starts bashing him with her teddy bear, screaming, 'What the fuck have you done with my things?' He makes a run for it and gets to his car, but she jumps onto the windscreen, yelling that she can't leave him now. He finally gets her off and screeches away. Back home with his family, Table calls the police to report the incident. But the police have already arrived at his front door, saying they've had complaints about his vehicle. With them is the strange little girl.

'It's possibly one of the best experiences I've had in a while,' Kylie said of the role. 'I think the biggest lesson I learnt with this is that I'm always nervous and anxious and excited about most projects. But with this one, I wanted the character to be so believable and she was so different to anything that I've come across. Although there was obviously a part in me that thought, Ah great, I can expand on that. Some madness somewhere.'

'She was wonderful,' enthused *Hayride to Hell*'s director, Kimble Rendall. 'She's a totally professional person to work with. She didn't balk at doing anything. I suggested if she wanted stunt people to double for things. She gets quite physical – jumping on the car, getting thrown off the car and running everywhere. But she did all that. She was just helpful and into it all the way through. Not a drama queen.

'I think she's a very good actress. Having spoken to other people who have worked with her, she's just totally one hundred per cent into whatever she does. And that's why she's so good at it.'

Kylie attested the character took over her life for the duration of filming. Working fourteen-hour days, she joked that the world ceased to exist for that week. 'Come the evening, there wasn't much time to switch off, so I was quite a beast for a while. My boyfriend was like, "Who is this girl?" I just think it's funny that I was pretty awful and I knew it but I didn't want to let go of her too much. Not that I went home and was being a complete lunatic.

But I guess that's work and that's completely understandable: You've got a job to do and your mind-set is that this time is set aside for the film.

'I guess every actor goes through that but this was the first time I experienced it to that degree. Such a good experience. I felt so inspired by it. Scared the life out of me but I think I did a reasonable job.'

Although it will probably never get a commercial release, *Hayride to Hell* was screened at the London Film Festival, the Chicago Underground Film Festival, and the Telluride Festival in the midwest of the USA. By the time she left Australia in March, Kylie still hadn't seen the final product.

Kylie spent most of her three months in Australia relaxing with her new boyfriend, a Zane O'Donnell lookalike called Mark Gerber. A former international model, Gerber had recently appeared as a blind and often naked stablehand alongside Sam Neill, Hugh Grant and Elle Macpherson, in the locally produced film, *Sirens.*

Their relationship started within weeks of Kylie arriving in Australia. When it became public, it was reported that the superstar had gone out of her way to find and seduce the statuesque 35-year-old, having taken an immediate liking to what she saw of him in *Sirens.* There was an element of truth in this, although Kylie and Gerber had previously met through mutual friends in Sydney.

The relationship began in earnest when Kylie invited Gerber to join her on an intimate cruise of Sydney Harbour. From then on, the two were regularly seen together around the city. On several occasions, Kylie was in the audience at gigs when Gerber played bass with his rock band, Flame Boa.

While local paparazzi took snaps of them shopping and having coffee around Bondi Beach, newspapers ran photos of the couple attending high-profile social events around town, such as the birthday bash of a local magazine and the opening of a Robert Mapplethorpe exhibition.

At the Mapplethorpe show, which was also attended by Bryan Ferry, Kylie and Gerber posed with Pierre et Gilles, the duo of artists famous for their highly stylised, gay iconic imagery. They were soon to use Kylie as the subject of one of their works. The piece would have Kylie dressed up as a nun to represent Mary MacKillop, the first Australian to be nominated for sainthood. Sitting on a carousel with three stuffed kangaroos on her lap, Kylie's glowing face was pointed skyward. 'I thought it was amazing that they pretty much got me in a nutshell,' Kylie would comment after seeing the finished work. 'That I do suffer a lot of guilt. And I do think I am the girl on the show pony sometimes. My best friend has described me as the girl at the circus on the pony, striking a pose.'

Another opening attended by Kylie and Gerber, this time of a more low-key nature, was an exhibition of artwork by Gerber's brother. Kylie's presence was a disruption, overshadowing the work on show. This didn't endear Kylie to the Gerber family, especially Mark's mother, an academic and feminist who had always been very protective of her boys. Even a brief holiday at the Gerbers' beach home after the exhibition didn't smooth over matters. 'I think the family were looking out for Mark a bit,' observed a friend of the Gerbers. 'They were a bit concerned that she might have a Mark in every port.'

As it panned out, the relationship only ended up surviving for the duration of Kylie's Australian holiday. A few months later, Kylie would explain, 'It's a long-distance romance and at the moment my work is so much at the forefront of everything I do, any relationship is really secondary. So it's not as it was, for no other reason than it's hard. You fool yourself into thinking this will work, but it is really difficult. Romance is wonderful and it's something I enjoy. I go on dates but I'm so content with my work,

I couldn't be happier. I don't know if I prefer being single or in relationships but I'm having a ball right now.'

For his part, Gerber would never publicly comment on the liaison further than stating, 'It's in the past now. You move on.' While the international gossip columns painted Gerber as devastated by the realisation that it was all over, his friends told a different story. One recounted that the relationship had been fatally destabilised by an argument in which Kylie posed the question to her lover, 'When are you going to do something with your life?' Kylie would later admit: 'I was always saying to him, "You've got to do more acting", bossy woman that I am.' Gerber, who had already secured spots in a couple of high-profile television ads and was busy working with his band, considered he was already doing his fair share with life.

Another friend's interpretation of Gerber's high-profile dalliance had a different thrust. 'The motherfucker's hung like a donkey,' he candidly explained. 'I think that's what it was about. It wasn't all it was made out to be. She's a pretty cute little blonde number and I think he just wanted to pop her but it got a little out of hand. And as soon as Mark's old girlfriend got back on the scene, he just bailed on Kylie. I think he thought, I'll have a bit of fun here, and then the papers got a hold of it and he was like, "It's not worth this much bullshit." He got plenty of nice jewellery and clothes and shit like that and then said, "See ya." '

Whatever the case, Kylie was soon back to playing international superstar and Mark Gerber had become just another name somewhere on page two of her list of ex-lovers.

By May 1995, Kylie was in Hollywood ready to work on a new movie. She had decided to take on the role of Petra, an Australian oceanographer, in a comedy called *Bio Dome*. Made by the same producers as the box-office hit *Dumb and Dumber*,

199

the film had her co-starring alongside Pauly Shore and Stephen Baldwin. While on set, Kylie pledged her enthusiasm for the new project. 'I laughed all the way through the script,' she said, 'and that was before I really knew much about Stephen and Pauly. With them together in this film, it's so much fun. I swear I've just loved it.

'We decided it was better for my character to be an Australian because it gives them more to play with. Pauly calls her "Petriedish" or "Barbie on the Shrimp" and I get to shoot him the filthiest looks when he jumps around like a kangaroo, so it's been fun.'

It was hardly surprising that once filming had finished and Kylie watched herself acting out jokes of that calibre on the big screen, her stance on the whole thing changed considerably. 'It's very frustrating because you don't get to perform unless you're the star,' she complained, distancing herself from the movie even before it had been released. 'I would love to do an independent film piece where the scenes made sense and there was a story and there could be some kind of progression. That's what I long for, acting-wise. I'm sure the right script will turn up but I'm not actively pursuing it.

'I've done two Hollywood films that have left me very disappointed and, seriously, I couldn't take another one. They were fun, lighthearted, and I did them for American exposure, but these Hollywood things are like, "Let's get her into something short and tight and do scenes that have very little relevance to each other." '

Kylie sensed she'd made a bad mistake in getting involved with this film about two dimwits who find themselves trapped in an environmentally controlled dome. Her judgement would prove to be correct. When *Bio Dome* was finally released into American cinemas for Christmas, it flopped. When it was time for the film to be released in Australia, its distributors decided to dump it straight on to video-store shelves.

While *Bio Dome* was being filmed, the tabloids were convinced that Kylie had a thing going with Shore, whose previous girlfriend had been the late porn star, Savannah. There were reports of Kylie moving into Shore's house in the Hollywood Hills and the two having weekends together in Las Vegas. But soon after work was completed, Kylie took off for a month, driving across the States in a '79 Trans-Am with a companion, future boyfriend Stephane Sednaoui. Kylie later described how she 'Went along old Route 66, called my dad up, very excited: "I'm on the same road that you went on." He did it in '58 and '61. It's the closest I've ever got to following in my father's footsteps. I talk about doing a lot of things and never really do them, so this was one under my belt.'

Kylie spent most of the rest of 1995 in London, back in low-profile mode. This didn't stop her face popping up in the tabloids' pages, whether she was shopping in Kings Road, buying vegies at the Portobello Road markets, or attending various public functions like the BAFTA awards at the London Palladium or a book launch held by designer Gianni Versace. Apart from her festival performances with Nick Cave, Kylie also made a couple of other live appearances. There was a one-off show on Ibiza and a guest spot during Elton John's set at a charity show at the Royal Albert Hall. With John dressed in drag and a blond wig, the two dueted on 'Sisters are Doing It for Themselves', the same song Kylie had sung years ago with sister Dannii, in her first live performance.

As 1995 drew to a close, Kylie looked towards starting work on a new album. There had already been meetings with Brothers in Rhythm, the producers responsible for much of 1994's *Kylie Minogue*, but Kylie's work with Cave had put a new concept into her head. 'My daytime fantasy,' she revealed, 'is to have an album where I can work with the likes of Blur and Nick Cave and some American artists, like ten different bands of all different styles, and just see what they would do with me. It would be like giving ten sculptors a piece of rock. It would mean a bit of a regression for me, because that [manipulation in the studio] is exactly what I was trying to escape from. But just as an experimental thing, it would be very interesting.'

IT'S THE LAST DAY OF 1996 AND THE 28-YEAR-OLD KYLIE, SPORTING A SHORT-CROPPED BRUNETTE HAIR-DO, REAPPEARS ON NEWSSTANDS AROUND AUSTRALIA FOR THE FIRST TIME IN WHAT FEELS LIKE AN ETERNITY.

EPILOGUE

still a star

Kylie's on the cover of a weekly women's magazine, *New Idea*. A few years back, Kylie swore she'd never again talk to such magazines because of the amount of fiction they'd printed about her since the start of her career. But this interview, supplemented by new studio photos straight from Terry Blamey's office, appears authentic enough.

For the most part, Kylie is asked about the usual things and provides her stock-standard answers. Yes, she's the one in control of her career now. Yes, she's rich but has no idea how rich (one report had her earn $650 000 in 1995). Yes, Michael Hutchence was the single greatest influence in her life.

Kylie also talks about her relationship with Stephane Sednaoui. 'Yes, I'm in love,' beams Kylie. 'Stephane is wonderful, adorable and inspirational. I need kindness, spontaneity and sincerity in a man and I've got all three in Stephane. Plus he's successful and driven too. I admire that.'

Kylie denies recent media reports that the two are about to wed. 'For me, I don't think there is such a thing as a perfect soul mate forever,' she says. 'Stephane is perfect for me at this time, but perhaps in a few years he might not be and that would be okay. I really believe that people go along parallel paths for a while and then one might veer off and run parallel with somebody else. I don't know why I think like this. Mum and Dad have been together for years and are still very much in love.'

It's now nearly a decade since Kylie walked on to the set of *Neighbours* for the first time. In those ten years, everything has changed, even if much of the world around Kylie still won't accept that. When the singer made a guest appearance on stage with Nick Cave at a music festival in Melbourne at the start of 1996, hecklers in the crowd took pride in chanting: 'Go back to Ramsay Street!' Reviews in the city's newspapers were still asking, 'Is it now cool to like Kylie?'

Kylie wouldn't have even noticed. For years now, she's had the respect of those who matter to her. One example: the first time Kylie appeared on the cover of the British style bible *Tatler*, back in 1988, the magazine mocked her as 'looking like a shop girl' with 'canine' features. When she graced *Tatler*'s cover again, late in 1995, the magazine was forced to admit that 'Kylie has achieved hip status. At almost thirty, she is still a star and shines ever more brightly.'

It is impossible to predict where Kylie's career might go from here. Since the start of the 1990s, each new step has magically presented itself to her out of thin air, Kylie rarely setting the agenda.

One thing for certain, her new record, *The Impossible Princess*, is scheduled for release late in 1997. Content aside (Nick Cave has contributed a song), its success will rely heavily on Kylie's willingness to get out and promote it hard, just like in the old days. Whether she can motivate herself to do the hard yards is questionable.

For years, Kylie has expressed a desire to crack the United States in a big way, but all her work to that end has come to nothing. Her recent experiences have turned her away from the Hollywood treadmill and it would now take a miracle for her music ever to make an impression on the charts there again.

Perhaps she should look towards her original craft, acting in television. How's Kylie living in Melrose Place as an idea?

Of course, her immensely successful career everywhere else has dramatically changed the lives of those who've been able to sustain a grip on her coat-tails. The most obvious example is Terry Blamey. As soon as Kylie based herself permanently in London, in 1990, Blamey dumped his family and followed her over.

Financed by Kylie's success, TBM – Terry Blamey Management – is now an international concern. Aside from acting as a model and actor agency, Blamey personally handles the careers of Dannii and another Australian expatriate, singer Gina G, who has enjoyed chart success in both the USA and UK. Blamey employs many of the same tactics he learnt from Kylie to keep his other talents' stars burning brightly by whatever means possible.

As Kylie moves into her second decade as an international performer, perhaps it's time she looked for someone with a little more creative nous to help guide her into the new millennium.

'What would I like to be remembered for?' pondered Kylie recently. 'I don't know. I hate trying to look at myself that objectively. Singing, that would be part of it, but it wouldn't be the whole shebang. Anything that comes to mind seems to be corny – a nice person, hard-working – so there's nothing I could be concise about. Just to be remembered would be nice.

'It can be quite depressing because I'm not brilliant at one thing. It's a mixture – I look all right, I can sing all right. I can dance reasonably well. People can relate to me because I'm not out of reach or unattainable. It's a kind of ordinariness. That sounds depressing, doesn't it?'

Perhaps, but it's that odinariness that has been the foundation of Kylie's appeal from the start. To many in the world, she will always remain the little miss stuck in a greater-than-life fantasy, the girl-next-door mystically and inexplicably chosen to live out the dreams of a generation.

In the early days, Kylie sent out the vibe that 'this could be you!' The millions of teeny-boppers who absorbed her every drama on *Neighbours* and bought her records by the chartful implicitly accepted this, and found it easy to project themselves on to such an attainable image. They worshipped that ordinariness.

But Kylie had to grow up. As her fame grew and her audience grew older, it was her tenacity and personal fortitude in the face of what seemed a barrage of media criticism and abuse that engendered loyalty.

Without question, Kylie's core audience – those who would consider purchasing any new Kylie product – has dramatically declined when compared to her heyday. But anyone who's ever bought a Kylie record retains at least a detached fascination with every tit-bit of information, every update of what's happening in the life of their old friend.

To many, Kylie will always remain Charlene from *Neighbours*, an image frozen in time that represents another age. Such people are living in the past.

Kylie Ann Minogue has become what the world demanded of her from the moment she stepped in front of a camera – a superstar, one of those blessed figures whose life appears so much more interesting and uncomplicated than our own. Kylie made the wish – the world insisted it come true.

Those still awaiting her fall from grace will have to wait another lifetime. The image of Kylie is with us forever. The shape it might take in the years to come is anybody's guess.

BIBLIOGRAPHY

primary sources

Gay Alcorn and Libby Webster, 'The Millionairess Next Door', *Herald*, 6/5/88

David Baird, 'Kylie Tells All', *Sun*, 18/5/88

Kim Langley, 'The Minogue Machine', *Sydney Morning Herald*, 1/4/88

Sasha Stone, 'Kylie Minogue: The Superstar Next Door', *MBI*, 1990

Sonya Voumard, 'Reaching for the Stars', *Herald*, 8/12/84

Andrew Watt, *Kylie Minogue*, ACP, 1987

secondary sources

Patricia Amad and Philippa Hawker, '*The Delinquents*', *Cinema Papers*, July 1989

Nick Cave and Kylie Minogue, 'Nick and Kylie Get Intimate', *Sydney Morning Herald*, 22/9/95

Toby Creswell, 'She's Gotta Have It', *Rolling Stone*, February 1991

Susan Crossley, 'Kylie's Come of Age', *The Daily Telegraph*, 22/12/89

Penelope DeBelle, 'Diva', *Sydney Morning Herald*, 23/7/94

Christie Eliezer, 'Kylie USM', *Juke*, 2/1/93

Christie Eliezer, 'Suicide Blonde', *Juke*, 22/12/90

George Epaminondas and Tom Doyle, 'Kylie on the Hop', *Elle*, March 1995

Michael Gow, 'In Bed with Jason', *Blue*, 1996

Chris Heath, 'Kylie's Cool World', *The Face*, June 1994

Jeff Jenkins, 'Me and My Music', *Sun*, 1/2/90

Tony Johnston, 'Fame at a Price', *Scene*, 6/12/86

Karen Kissane, 'Soaps: More Bubble than Trouble', *Time*, 25/4/88

'Kylie Minogue's Brave New Whirl', *Follow Me*, January 1990

Peter Lalor, 'Our Girl Kylie's No. 1', *Sun*, 16/2/88

John Lyons, 'I Should be so Credible', *Good Weekend*, 15/12/90

David Meech, 'The Happy Kylie Show', *Campaign*, August 1994

Sian Pattenden, 'Whenever You're Ready Love', *Select*, September 1994

Rosalind Reines, 'The Price of Fame', *Mode*, September 1989

Frank Robson, 'Kylie: A Serious Story', *The Australian Magazine*, 8/7/89

Katherine Tulich, 'It Just Happened', *Sun-Herald*, 7/1/90

Peter Wilmoth, 'Jason, Seriously', *The Sunday Age*, 23/4/95

other sources

The Official Kylie Annual – 1990, 1991

DISCOGRAPHY

albums

kylie   july, 1988

'I Should be so Lucky'
'The Loco-Motion'
'Je Ne Sais Pas Pourquoi'
'It's No Secret'
'Got to be Certain'
'Turn It into Love'
'I Miss You'
'I'll Still be Loving You'
'Look My Way'
'Love at First Sight'

enjoy yourself   october, 1989

'Hand on Your Heart'
'Wouldn't Change a Thing'
'Never Too Late'
'Nothing to Lose'
'Tell Tale Signs'
'My Secret Heart'
'I'm Over Dreaming (Over You)'

'Tears on My Pillow'
'Heaven and Earth'
'Enjoy Yourself'

rhythm of love   november, 1990

'Better the Devil You Know'
'Step Back in Time'
'What Do I Have to Do?'
'Secrets'
'Always Find the Time'
'The World Still Turns'
'Shocked'
'One Boy Girl'
'Things Can Only Get Better'
'Count the Days'
'Rhythm of Love'

213

let's get to it   october, 1991

'Word Is Out'
'Just Give Me a Little More Time'
'Too Much of a Good Thing'
'Finer Feelings'
'If You Were with Me Now'
'Let's Get to It'
'Right Here, Right Now'
'Live and Learn'
'No World Without You'
'I Guess I Like It Like That'

greatest hits   october, 1992

'I Should be so Lucky'
'Got to be Certain'
'The Loco-Motion'
'Je Ne Sais Pas Pourquoi'
'Especially for You'
'Turn It into Love'
'It's No Secret'
'Hand on Your Heart'
'Wouldn't Change a Thing'
'Never Too Late'
'Tears on My Pillow'
'Better the Devil You Know'
'Step Back in Time'
'What Do I Have to Do'
'Shocked'
'Word is Out'
'If You Were with Me Now'
'Give Me Just a Little More Time'
'Finer Feelings'
'What Kind of Fool'
'Where in the World'
'Celebration'

kylie minogue   november, 1994

'Confide in Me'
'Surrender'
'If I was Your Lover'
'Where is the Feeling'
'Put Yourself in My Place'

'Dangerous Game'
'Automatic Love'
'Where Has the Love Gone?'
'Falling'
'Time Will Pass You By'

the impossible princess   late 1997

singles

'Locomotion'/'Glad to be Alive' July, 1987 – Australia only

'I Should be so Lucky'/'I Should be so Lucky' (instrumental)
  January, 1988

'Got to be Certain'/'Got to be Certain' June, 1988   215

'The Loco-Motion'/'I'll Still be Loving You' July, 1988

'Je Ne Sais Pas Pourquoi'/'Made in Heaven' October, 1988

'Especially for You'/'All I Wanna Do is Make You Mine' (with Jason
  Donovan) November, 1988

'Turn It into Love'/'Made in Heaven' December, 1988 – Japan
  only

'It's No Secret'/'Made in Heaven' February, 1989 – Japan, USA,
  NZ only

'Hand on Your Heart'/'Just Wanna Love You' April, 1989

'Wouldn't Change a Thing'/'It's No Secret' July, 1989

'Never Too Late'/'Made in Heaven' October, 1989

'Tears on My Pillow'/'We Know the Meaning of Love' January,
  1990

'Better the Devil You Know'/'I'm Over Dreaming (Over You)' May,
  1990

'Step Back in Time'/'Step Back in Time' (instrumental) October,
  1990

'What Do I Have to Do?'/'What Do I Have to Do?' (instrumental) January, 1991

'Shocked'/'Shocked' May, 1991

'Word Is Out'/'Say the Word – I'll Be There' August, 1991

'If You Were with Me Now' (with Keith Washington)/'I Guess I Like It Like That' October, 1991

'Give Me Just a Little More Time'/'Do You Dare' January, 1992

'Finer Feelings'/'Closer' April, 1992

'What Kind of Fool'/'Things Can Only Get Better' August, 1992

'Celebration'/'Too Much of a Good Thing' December, 1992

'Confide in Me'/'Where Has the Love Gone?' October, 1994

'Put Yourself in My Place' January, 1995

'Where is the Feeling' August, 1995

'Where the Wild Roses Grow' (with Nick Cave) October, 1995

compilations

Kylie's Remixes
Kylie's Remixes Volume 2
Kylie Non-Stop History 50+1
Greatest Remix Hits Volume 1
Greatest Remix Hits Volume 2
All were released in 1993.

videos

The Kylie Collection 1988
The Videos 2 1989
Kylie on the Go 1991
Let's Get to It – The Videos 1992
Live in Dublin 1992
Greatest Hits 1992

LIST OF PHOTOGRAPHS

black and white

1 An early photo of Kylie's mother, Carol, showing a remarkable resemblance to her famous daughter.

2 Baby Kylie.

3 A lighting-test Polaroid of the 17-year-old Kylie on the set of *Fame and Misfortune*, in 1985.

4 + **5** Kylie as the conniving sister, Sam, in *Fame and Misfortune*, with co-stars Myles Collins and Peter Hosking.

217

6 At the height of her fame in *Neighbours*, Kylie poses on a Sydney street in a wondrous eighties creation.

7 Kylie greets thousands of fans at a shopping centre in Sydney the day before Scott and Charlene's wedding on *Neighbours*, in July 1987.

8 Kylie and American actor Charlie Schlatter, her co-star in *The Delinquents*, at a press conference in 1989.

9 Kylie meets Princess Diana after the Bicentennial concert at Sydney's Entertainment Centre in 1988.

10 Kylie steps out with her new lover, Michael Hutchence, at the premiere of *The Delinquents* in late 1989.

11 Kylie and Michael in love, 1990. (Photo by Robert Rose)

12 The couple out in Sydney on Michael's Harley Davidson. (Photo by John Dearfield)

13 Nick Cave and Kylie at Heathrow in 1995. (Photo by John Cheves)

colour

1 Kylie and her mother, Carol, in 1987.
(Photo by Greg Noakes)

2 The 19-year-old star on her first visit to London in 1987.
(Photo by S&G)

3 Kylie at home in Melbourne with the family dog, Gabby, 1987.
(Photo by Greg Noakes)

4 Kylie in a SAW publicity shot, about 1988.

5 A 1988 publicity shot for Kylie's new single, 'Got to be Certain'.

6 Kylie and *Neighbours* co-stars Jason Donovan and Peter O'Brien
present an award at the 1988 Countdown music awards.
(Photo by Greg Noakes)

7 Kylie and Jason perform at the Royal Variety Children's
Show in London in 1989. (Photo by Tim Hall)

8 + 9 Kylie on stage at Wembley in John Galliano's controversial outfits.
(Photos by Mick Hutson and Jim Steele)

10 Kylie struts her stuff at a Gay Pride concert in London, 1991.
(Photo by Joe Ramsay)

11 A glamorous Kylie around the time of the release of her
album, *Kylie Minogue*, in 1994. (Photo by Monique March)

12 Kylie wows the crowd in a Versace dress at a party in 1995.
(Photo by UPPA)

13 Kylie in 'rave' mode in 1996. (Photo by Michael Putland)

ACKNOWLEDGEMENTS

hand on your heart thanks

Un ringraziamento amorevole alla famiglia Scatena – papa Domenico, mama Ovidia e` fratello Bruno. Per il vostro continuo sostegno affetto.

To my beautiful girl Rachel. I still don't understand how you put up with everything. Love always, Bubba.

To Enio. For saving my sanity once again.

Great thanks also to: Emily Ross, Angus Holland, Jeff Jenkins, Christos, Skye, Rhys, the Doctor, the Newmans, Sean, Jo, Marco, El, Toby, Rose and all at Cameron Creswell. An extra special thanks to the Penguin chicks for letting me push your patience without calling in the cops.

Finally, thank you, Kylie Ann Minogue. May the world continue to bring you only the most wonderful of experiences.

INDEX

index